TURBOCHARGE
YOUR
TEACHING

By
Joanne Belizaire

Turbocharge Your Teaching

Author: Joanne Belizaire

Copyright © 2025 J. Belizaire

The right of J. Belizaire to be identified as author of this work has been asserted by the author in accordance with section 77 and 78 of the Copyright, Designs and Patents Act 1988.

ISBN 978-1-83538-442-8 (Paperback)
     978-1-83538-443-5 (Hardback)
     978-1-83538-444-2 (E-Book)

Cover Design by: Fiverr

Book Layout by:
    White Magic Studios
    www.whitemagicstudios.co.uk

Published by:
    Maple Publishers
    Fairbourne Drive, Atterbury,
    Milton Keynes,
    MK10 9RG, UK
    www.maplepublishers.com

A CIP catalogue record for this title is available from the British Library. All rights reserved. No part of this book may be reproduced or translated by any form or by any means, electronic or mechanical, including photocopying, recording or by any information storage and retrieval system without written permission from the author.
The views expressed in this work are solely those of the author and do not necessarily reflect the views of the publisher, and the publisher hereby disclaims any responsibility for them.

Acknowledgements

I would like to thank my husband, who has always championed me and been my steadfast supporter, and my family and friends for encouraging me in all my endeavours.

I would also like to extend my thanks to students (past and present) for their enthusiasm, honest feedback and questioning – all of you have played a part in my on-going teaching journey.

May I also take this opportunity to thank supportive colleagues, who have been generous in sharing their knowledge, expertise and time, as well as the kind souls, visionaries and all sorts of practitioners within education who have influenced my thinking about teaching and learning.

Dedication

To Dadra, grandad, Jean and Peter who are forever remembered and forever loved.

Introduction

Are you considering teaching and want to take a behind-the-scenes peek into the life of a Key Stage 2 primary school teacher? Are you beginning a career in teaching and want to feel prepared for the start of September? Or perhaps you are an experienced teacher who is looking for a refresher in alternative ways to **simplify**, **streamline** and **systematise** your practice to reduce stress and make life easier and more enjoyable for you and your pupils? If so, **Turbocharge Your Teaching** is for you, offering valuable insights regardless of your career stage.

The ideas expressed in this guidebook are principally about **reducing** workload, **enhancing** learning outcomes, and **optimising** productivity. The content has emerged and developed from my two decades of teaching experience. Not all ideas are my own as I have picked up various tricks of the trade throughout the years and adapted them to suit me. This book, pragmatic rather than pedagogical or academic in tone, features authentic tried-and-tested strategies and practical suggestions that can be applied immediately in the classroom; in other words, this book will provide you with the path of least resistance by furnishing you with real-world teaching tools so you can be confident in your daily practice. It is my hope that this book is a one-stop resource which will allow you to hit the ground running.

This guide is not concerned with the latest behaviour management strategies as there are many books which already explore such themes in depth elsewhere. Instead, it cuts to the chase and delves into the **not-so-obvious** realities of teaching, such as red flags to look out for when seeking employment; teacher organisation; lesson slides; email composition; equipment to buy for the classroom; setting up the classroom environment to maximise learning; and practical, methodical approaches to lesson planning – all of which you can implement straightaway.

I have always enjoyed sharing good practice with colleagues to help students to flourish, learn and grow, and I hope that this guidebook allows me to do this on a wider scale. I am by no means the finished article as I continue to strive to be a better teacher, and I'm sure you will build on or tweak what I have poured into here. Every day is a school day! Time is precious in teaching, and I want this book to save you oodles of time. With this in mind, each chapter is accessible and can be read in isolation, so you can dip in and out easily.

1. **Chapter 1: A Teacher's Treasure Trove: Tools of the Trade** is about the physical tools of the classroom, such as storage solutions, items to make your life a whole lot easier. Think of this chapter as mental house cleaning which will give you the time to concentrate on what matters – you and the children.

2. **Chapter 2: Searching for Teaching Jobs and Spotting Red Flags** considers how best to find an effective school and poses a series of essential questions for you to answer before completing your application form.

3. **Chapter 3: Top Ten Supply Teaching Hacks** provides ten top tips for those who are entering the world of supply teaching.

4. **Chapter 4: Drop Dazzling Displays!** This chapter focuses on how to create easy-to-manage, labour-efficient display boards by providing purposeful step-by-step content for your boards.

5. **Chapter 5: Awesome Organisation** outlines routines and templates to reduce workload and optimise learning.

6. **Chapter 6: Smarter Marking** explores ways in which teacher marking can be reduced without compromising on the quality of feedback to pupils. This chapter includes

a range of strategies, such as secretarial codes and motivational stickers and stamps, and places the onus on pupils to monitor and actively evaluate the quality of their work to improve their educational outcomes.

7. **Chapter 7: Have Yourself a Terrific Transition Day!** In this chapter, I provide a roadmap for Transition Day preparation which dissects one of my typical Transition Days so that it serves as a practical step-by-step guide which you can use straightaway.
8. **Chapter 8: Principles of Lesson Planning** gives a detailed account of lesson planning, and the resourcing involved.
9. **Chapter 9: Watchful Eyes** is concerned with inspections and observations and how best to handle uncomfortable scrutiny.
10. **Chapter 10: Meetings: The Thieves of Time** addresses the pros and cons of school meetings and how to approach them.
11. **Chapter 11: Assemblies** explains the format I use when preparing and delivering schoolwide assemblies.
12. **Chapter 12: Conclusion** summarises my general thoughts about teaching and what I hoped to achieve by writing this short book.

Inside, you will find overviews, frameworks, examples, tables, templates, photographs (please forgive the quality of some of the pictures as many were hastily taken during busy working days), and references to lesson planning to support you in your teaching practice. I suggest that you read this book with a pen, pencil or highlighter in hand so you can annotate the text; there is also additional space for you to write on the blank pages provided.

Teaching certainly has its downsides because it can be gruelling due to an ever-increasing workload, worsening pupil behaviour and a worrying increase in adversarial parents. The teaching profession is a beast that definitely needs to be tamed as there is a great deal of waffle embedded in education (which wastes valuable time), unhelpful initiatives (that have little or no impact on learning), undue pressure (namely, excessive scrutiny), and external interference which, although often well-meaning, can create more confusion because each expert who visits wants to put their stamp on how the school moves forward.

Despite these negatives, teaching is certainly not all gloom and doom as there really is no other vocation like teaching; it can be enormously exciting because you play a huge role in positively transforming the hearts and minds of future generations and, in the right school, you have a certain level of autonomy. Being a teacher always gives you the opportunity to learn new skills, too. I would also like to add that I have had many happy moments in the classroom and at the end of the academic year, I am moved by the kind words from students and parents as well as the thank you cards and gifts.

Thank you for purchasing this book; I do hope that you find it a good investment. Now that you have **Turbocharge Your Teaching** in the palm of your hands, let's dive right in!

CONTENTS

Acknowledgements 3

Dedication 4

Introduction 5

Chapter 1 – A Teacher's Treasure Trove: Tools of the Trade 13
- Minimalism: The Rationale Behind this Chapter 14
- Trusty Tools 15
- Other Useful Teaching Equipment 45

Chapter 2 – Searching for Teaching Jobs and Spotting Red Flags 66
- Changing States of Schools 67
- Online Presence 68
- Headteachers 72
- SEND Provision 73
- Data and Ofsted 74
- Touring the School 76
- Wellbeing is Not Cake and One-off Events! 82
- Behaviour 85
- Behaviour Policies 86
- Type of School and Training Opportunities 87
- Go with Your Gut! 89

Chapter 3 – Top Ten Supply Teaching Hacks 94
- Hack 1: Travel & School 95
- Hack 2: Arrival & Resources 95
- Hack 3: Register 97
- Hack 4: Disclosure Barring Service (DBS) 97
- Hack 5: Set the Tone 98
- Hack 6: Stationery 98

- Hack 7: Textbooks......99
- Hack 8: Marking......100
- Hack 9: Visualiser & USB Stick......101
- Hack 10: Handover Notes & Tidying......103

Chapter 4 – Drop Dazzling Displays!......105
- Look Around Your Classroom......108
- Classroom Display Materials......111
- Corridor Display Boards......125

Chapter 5 – Awesome Organisation......129
- Alarms......129
- Before Work......130
- Get Into a Work Routine......130
- During Lessons......131
- During Break......132
- During Lunch......132
- Batch and Spread!......132
- Maximise PPA......133
- After School......134
- Keyboard Shortcuts......134
- Get Friendly with the Photocopier!......135
- Emails......135
- Electronic Bookmarks & Pinning......140
- Reading Records......141
- Laptop Usage......141
- Christmas Resources......141
- Electronic Folder Organisation......142
- Templates......143
- PowerPoint Templates......144
- Life Admin......154

Chapter 6 – Smarter Marking 158
- Proofreading Symbols 158
- Live Marking 160
- Self and Peer Assessment 160
- High-quality Language 161
- Open Books 161
- Sticky Index Tabs Page Markers 162
- Precise Learning Objectives and Success Criteria 162
- Assessment 164
- Homework 164
- Stamps & Stickers 165
- Numbering Books 166
- Sampling 166

Chapter 7 – Have Yourself a Terrific Transition Day! 169
- Preparation: The Day Before 15:45–16:15 170
- Arrival 171
- Housekeeping 175
- Structure of the Day 177

Chapter 8 – Principles of Lesson Planning 200
- Educational Investments 202
- Headspace for Planning 205
- Mechanics of Lesson Planning 208
- English Planning for a Unit of Work Example | Descriptive Writing | Duration: One week 213

Chapter 9 – Watchful Eyes 226
- Daily Practice 227
- Don't Look! 228
- Feedback 230

Chapter 10 – Meetings: The Thieves of Time 233
- Staff Meetings/Training 235
- Good Practice 236
- Disciplinary Meetings 237
- Parental Meetings 238
- Key Points to Remember 239

Chapter 11 – Assemblies 243
- Preparing for General Assemblies 244
- Preparing for Class Assemblies 245
- Preparing for Celebration Assemblies 247

Chapter 12 – Conclusion 250

Appendices 251

Glossary of Acronyms 259

Useful References 261

Chapter 1
A Teacher's Treasure Trove: Tools of the Trade

The fictional character of the magical, calm and composed nanny Mary Poppins is who springs to mind whenever I think of someone having something for every occasion. In the classroom, having some key tools available will make your teaching life easier and enable you to be cool, calm, collected and adaptable when things do not go to plan, because you will have a range of helpful items at your disposal. By having your tools methodically organised, you'll avoid decision fatigue, too, and be able to set up and run a tight ship. More importantly, feeling prepared builds confidence.

Teaching is a complex role that demands a great deal of physical and mental energy, and the start of a new academic year is usually frantic, and all systems are go! This section of the book is a comprehensive inventory that will allow you to resource your classroom effectively. Consider this chapter as your comfort blanket, your grab-and-go bag which automates crucial aspects of your teaching as soon as you set foot in the classroom. I purchased many of the items discussed in this chapter over time and have, therefore, steadily built up a bank of my own resources throughout my teaching career, but your school may already have some of the items featured here or the budget to provide them for you.

Teachers are strapped for time; therefore, it makes sense to invest time at the outset to save time later down the road. If you can set up your classroom during part of the summer holiday, it will pay dividends because prior preparation, especially erecting backing paper and classroom displays, allows you to start the year in a more relaxed manner, as you won't feel rushed and stressed, trying to set up your classroom during INSET (In-service Training). INSET should be spent concentrating on the school's vision for the academic year; talking to your colleagues about lesson planning, seating plans and pupils; and photocopying and guillotining your resources for the week ahead.

Minimalism: The Rationale Behind this Chapter

"Less is more."

"Simplicity is beautiful."

"Do less, better."

These golden words form the basis of this chapter: **minimalism**. Applying a simple, minimalist approach to all aspects of teaching will allow you to maximise efficiency and boost your brain power and energy for the delivery of lessons. Being minimalist will give you clarity of thought and allow you to decisively reject what is redundant and strip back to the essentials.

It is easy to become indoctrinated into superficial ways of thinking in schools, particularly if the school in which you work has a culture of style over substance which advocates over-the-top classroom displays, pretty PowerPoints or teaching initiatives that lack depth; however, actively paring down what you do in your teaching practice will improve learning outcomes and enhance your professional life. Even if you're not minimalist by nature, I strongly urge you to adopt **simplicity** and **minimalism** in your classroom, because then you won't be overcomplicating matters or desperately trying to locate items by wading through excessive teaching-related clutter. A minimalist classroom also means that your classroom won't be visually cluttered, distracting, overstimulating or too colourful. Furthermore, you will not need a removal van to transport your items if or when you move to another classroom or school.

A messy classroom, such as one where every surface is covered by mountains of paper with books haphazardly arranged and a collection of pens and pencils strewn across the floor, gives a poor first impression to visitors. More importantly, it sends out the wrong subliminal message to pupils: the teacher is disorganised and doesn't care enough to make the workspace an inviting environment in which to work. In other words, pupils feel (albeit not perhaps consciously) unwelcome and unvalued.

Don't be a teacher magpie! Every fortnight, be evaluative and ruthless by getting rid of items that failed to add anything to the learning of your pupils or fulfil your own needs. If in doubt, throw it out! You and your pupils deserve to work in a pleasant environment that is not overwhelmed by mess and unnecessary teaching supplies. A warm, welcoming orderly environment is good for everyone's wellbeing.

Trusty Tools

The Delightful Diary

It goes without saying that schools are fast-paced and incredibly busy workplaces, and sometimes you feel as if you're just managing to stay on top of urgent deadlines and important dates. I have tried many different methods and newfangled ideas over the years to help me manage the recording of school-related tasks and information; for example, I used to use colour-coded **electronic Sticky Notes** on my computer desktop. I would colour-code the Post-it notes, too: pink for urgent items, green for non-urgent, and blue for items that were required within a set period but not urgent. This was fine whilst I had my laptop switched on, but not great when an idea randomly popped into my head and my laptop was switched off and in my bag. I always took the time to retrieve the laptop and switch it on whenever I had an idea because I wanted to centralise my ideas and tasks in one place rather than have them scattered around in different places, but it was a pain to have to record all information on my laptop.

In more recent years, in my quest to go **paperless**, I used my own small tablet with *Microsoft Word* installed. I had a Word file named 'Action List' and had it open throughout the day. I created a colour-coded daily checklist on it, but I was sometimes fretful about leaving it on my desk at school for fear of theft, and it lost its charge rather quickly. I soon discovered that I was far slower at writing with the stylus or my finger on the tablet and did not keep this method up for long.

Google Drive has some handy, accessible features, such as ***Google Keep*** and ***Google Tasks*** – all of which can be easily accessed on your phone so you can record your ideas on the go, but the majority of schools do not allow teachers to have their mobile phones out on desks in full view of students; therefore, quick access to *Google* may not be easy in the classroom, especially if your laptop doubles up as the main classroom computer due to the absence of an in-situ classroom computer, and you don't want the fuss of freezing the interactive board screen or toggling through an HDMI splitter just to add a quick note to your list.

So, what do I use now? Well, it's very low-tech and minimalist and involves a good old pen and some paper...it is...a hardback **A5 page-a-day diary**. I have found that this diary is the most useful item for recording key information and planning notes.

Yes, it's a bit bland and boring, a bit vanilla but it works! I have been using this approach for years and it has not failed me yet. A diary of this type is sturdy, durable, portable and does not require charging, unplugging or a battery. In a nutshell, no frills, no hassle, no fuss. Some schools provide spiral-bound **Teacher Planners** which many classroom practitioners find useful because they contain pre-filled headings, blank mark book templates, timetable templates and space to write lesson plans; however, by having blank pages, you can customise accordingly to suit your own needs. Nowadays, for the most part, schools expect pupils to be tracked electronically on a centralised computerised system; therefore, I no longer maintain a mark book manually except for the recording of homework. With the **A5 page-a-day diary**, each page is free of headings and unnecessary embellishments and the pages do not fall out as easily as they do with spiral-bound planners.

Before the start of the academic year, I purchase an **A5 page-a-day diary**. If A5 is too small for your needs, A4 versions of this type of diary are available. If you use an **A5 page-a-day diary**, you can put a **journal bandolier** on it.

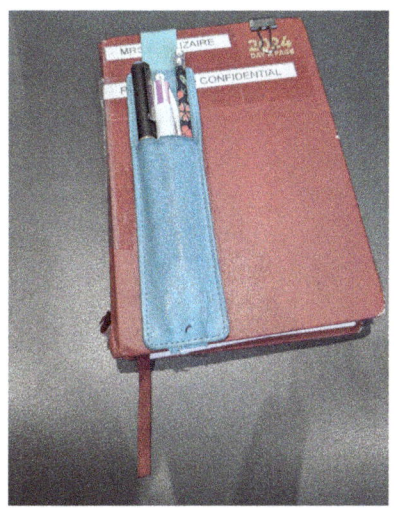

Picture 1: Journal Bandolier

Personally, I like having sufficient space to write and I tend to use my diary to centralise most of my teaching tasks, such as the recording of lesson planning ideas, deadlines, important dates and notes from training and staff briefings.

If you want to include a **yearly overview** of your school's academic year, you could download a copy from *Calendarpedia* at www.calendarpedia.co.uk and add dates from your school's diary. This can then be glued into the back of your diary – again, this means that you have key information stored in one place. I find this very useful as I can see what is happening each day at a glance. If your school already provides a calendar like that of *Calendarpedia*, then you won't have to do this. This website currently offers a range of UK calendar templates for free in *Word*, *Excel* and *PDF*. I also glue in a minimised copy of my timetable so that it fits neatly into the back of my diary.

You could generate your own priority codes; for example: ! or asterisk (*) for urgent items, or **colour coding**, such as traffic lighting, with highlighters. With my diary being A5, it compels me to be concise; therefore, I do not need additional notebooks for briefing, training or planning. This is also better for my shoulders and back as I do not have the heavy burden of physically carrying multiple folders and notebooks around with me.

Last year, I purchased a copy from *The Works* (other diaries are available) for less than £5 – I love a bargain! One of the first things I do is label my diary with my name using my *Dymo* label machine (other label printers are available, which I will discuss in more depth later), and I also ensure that a **'Private & Confidential'** label is clearly affixed to the front to deter any prying eyes. I also write my name inside. These labels have strong adhesive, look professional and are easy to apply, but a standard address label, if you do not have access to a *Dymo* maker, will also suffice. Nothing else adorns the front cover as this is time-consuming and not essential. Remember, don't congest your 'to do list' with unnecessary tasks.

Regarding private and confidential matters, to avoid GDPR (General Data Protection Regulation) breaches, do not write the names of pupils in your diary and ensure that language used is professional. For example, if you're writing lesson evaluations in your diary, avoid writing content, such as: ***Example 1:*** "Joe Bloggs is bone idle! He needs to be watched like a hawk next lesson!" Instead, it is better to write something along the following lines: ***Example 2:*** "Check in with JB regularly next lesson due to lack of work output." The second example uses initials and avoids using pronouns. The same principle goes for any member of the school community. No matter how tempting it might be to vent on a frustrating day, it must be remembered that this is not a personal journal, and it is imperative to write in a business-like manner. If your diary should go 'walkies', you can rest assured that you will not land you or your school in hot water.

You could also assign numbers to your students (that only you know) and use these assigned numbers instead. For certain evaluations, you could insert **time-saving codes, such as numbers (1-4) or colour key** for effort, understanding and performance; for example: green = underperforming pupil did not understand subject matter; pink = pupil partially understood; purple = fully understood, or use **traffic-light colours**. Alternatively, evaluations could be **one, two or three sides of a triangle** to indicate the extent to which the learning objective has been met by each pupil; this triangle shortcut is common in many schools now. Devising your own memorable **shortcuts** saves you having to write at length, which saves you time. You've worked hard all day, marking, attending meetings and should not have to write reams after having already put in so many hours. You are entitled to rest and deserve to have a life outside of school.

Even though I have the school year mapped out in my *Calendarpedia* document, I still quickly write key dates in the diary lightly in pencil to commit to memory what is happening across the week. I use pencil for the simple reason that if events change (as they often do in schools), I can neatly erase. If you are not provided with a hard copy of the school diary at the start of the academic year, you can often access it on your school's website, as most schools provide calendar dates to parents via their website.

In my diary, I also include **notice periods**. One never starts working in a school with immediate intentions of leaving; however, it is important to keep your options open and having the notice periods to hand is always a good idea for ease of reference. For your convenience, I have listed the current school term notice periods in the UK here:

If you wish to leave your job, you would be expected to give notice by the following dates:

- to leave on 31st December, formally give notice by no later than 31st October
- to leave on 30th April, formally give notice by no later than 28th February; and

- to leave on 31st August, formally give notice by no later than 31st May

I also **vertically divide the diary pages (with a pencil and ruler)** into two distinct sections to show teaching-related tasks at school and teaching tasks to be done at home. For any task that is urgent, I use a pink highlighter and tick off the task in pencil or cross out once completed and... voilà! That's it. After so much trial and error, this simple, low-maintenance option has been the most effective in organising my teaching workload. Here is an example of how I set out school tasks in my diary:

Friday 8th November 2024	
❏ Complete IEPs (deadline looming!) ❏ Write up certificates. ❏ Print off tomorrow's resources for RE.	**School Tasks at Home** ❏ Mark English books. ❏ Draft Science Week letter for the office.

I also include memory prompts (that only I would know) for my **school passwords** and suggest that you develop prompts to help you to remember passwords. For quickness, I write these inside the back cover of the diary. This is something that I felt compelled to do as many schools no longer have in-house full-time IT support, which means you cannot always afford to forget key passwords. **Warning:** Do not use the same password for different websites or IT systems, and do not leave passwords or usernames within view of others, such as on a Post-it note. I learned about a GDPR breach from completing a cybersecurity course, where a student found his teacher's login details on a Post-it note attached to the monitor and, because the teacher concerned had used the same login details for all educational sites, the student was able to access his teacher's computer to change his predicted GCSE grades. He also accessed his peers' contact details, too.

One of the key things to remember is that, as a teacher, it is important that you try to **simplify**, **streamline** and **systematise** your practice as much as you can; this will free and sharpen your mind, reduce stress and allow you to spend time exploring the more enjoyable aspects of teaching, such as developing your teaching practice through professional learning, nurturing a positive rapport with your class, and creating meaningful lessons for your pupils. Even if you decide against using a diary, **pick one place** where you can track many of your tasks and priorities, as this will make your life more manageable. A **page-a-day diary** is not particularly revolutionary, but its **simplicity** is what makes it effective. Furthermore, having only one A5-sized page per day focuses the mind to write succinctly.

If you're interested in knowing how I record my **personal** diary events, I insert them into my **phone calendar** and **colour-code** according to type of event, for example:

- **Yellow** – Holidays
- **Light orange** – Fun events/outings
- **Dark orange** – Medical appointments
- **Red** – Important personal dates; for example: car insurance, cancellation of subscriptions, renewals, etc.
- **Purple** – Chores/work reminders
- **Blue** – Birthday reminders

Dynamic Dymo Label Maker

The *Dymo Maker* is well-known in the world of electrics but perhaps less so in educational circles. More often used in the world of electrics for labelling fuse boards and cables, this fabulous, lightweight hand-held device is one of my teaching staples.

It is time efficient as multiple labels can be printed off at the touch of a button. The labels can be applied to most surfaces and are durable and easy to wipe.

Picture 2: Label Maker

Assuming that you will be provided with a school laptop when you start your teaching employment, always ensure that you label the laptop and battery supply provided by the school with your name, as it is easy to confuse laptops with those of your colleagues when they all look the same at first glance. Labelling is especially helpful during the school's annual Portable Appliance Testing (PAT) when all the laptop power supplies may be required to be left in a room for the PAT engineer. My other tip would be to ensure that you attach a bag charm or key ring to the laptop bag to make it easily identifiable.

When devising a seating plan, you may wish to label different table groups according to a topic, figure of history or colour. After the height of COVID-19 passed, I did not return to the table group arrangement and stuck with rows, as I found that behaviour was better. I used to have a coloured label for each row for the purpose of dismissing the class row by row but found that the labels would be tampered with by pupils or come off with time and look scrappy; so now I discreetly place numbered *Dymo* labels on the outside table legs – much quicker and easier than making a coloured label.

The pupils don't tamper with the labels because they are not visible to them, and I can quickly identify each numbered row with ease.

In the past, I word-processed pupils' names onto colourful pencil-themed labels I found on *Twinkl* and then proceeded to laminate and carefully cut around each label but not anymore; instead, I affix small *Dymo* labels bearing pupils' names on the front of their trays. I find 12mm black on white label tape works well. These *Dymo* labels fit perfectly onto the trays and stay fairly neat throughout the year, especially if you place clear labels over them. I also repeat this process for the labelling of cloakroom lockers and *Accelerated Reader* book bands.

There needs to be a strong reason behind everything you do as a teacher, and some teacher tasks, such as searching for or making eye-catching classroom labels, present no benefits. The *Dymo* labels are not pretty or eye-catching but so what? No pupil has ever complained to me about their tray label being boring because it is not important. Each pupil knows which tray belongs to them and that's all that is required. In short, less is more.

Dymo labels are also fantastic for labelling the placement of exercise books on your bookshelves and can be done in minutes – there is no need to find or make attractive labels. These simple labels make the location and designation of exercise books a breeze for my classroom book monitors. To reinforce the labels and prevent curling caused by the frequent removal and return of exercise books, I apply clear sticky labels over them to provide additional protection.

I also use the *Dymo Maker* to label whiteboard pens, cupboards (for example, my 'Wet Play' and 'Art' cupboards), teaching stamps, electronic cables and copies of my own textbooks. There are different options for the sizing of your lettering and there is a built-in mini guillotine to snip off your labels, so scissors are not necessary. My family and colleagues joke that I would label everything in sight if I could; that's how much I truly love this machine. All it needs are batteries and a label cartridge and you're ready to rock and roll!

Wonderful Whiteboard Pens

In general, schools provide whiteboard pens. There are many whiteboard pens on the market; however, Pentel Maxiflo Liquid Ink Drywipe markers are my go-to because the quality of the ink is good, and they have a pump at the end of the pen that can be depressed to replenish the ink. From personal experience, they are a good investment as they last longer than most other brands I have tried.

Worthwhile Washing Up Liquid

It is imperative that staff model tidiness and pride in all things to instil these qualities in the children. Having a clean classroom whiteboard on which to write is vital for learning. Children unconsciously pick up on disorder in the classroom and will subliminally mimic what they see; therefore, if your whiteboard is heavily stained, your desk is piled high with mountains of paperwork and miscellaneous mess or you frequently lose things, don't be surprised if your class begins to mirror this. Tidy space, tidy minds!

Using washing up liquid is a tip from one of the kind cleaners in a previous school where I worked, who noticed that I was struggling to thoroughly clean my whiteboard at the end of the day. She immediately took out her damp cloth, soaked with washing up liquid, and wiped it away in seconds. It worked a treat and now my board remains in tip-top sparkling condition as this is what I sometimes do at the end of the working day for stubborn stains. I don't have to do this often because keeping on top of cleaning prevents ink stain build-up and makes whiteboard cleaning generally easier. Whiteboard cleaning fluid can be used, too, but from my personal experience, washing up liquid (any brand) is just as effective, requires less effort and a little goes a long way.

The Fantastic Foldback Clip

These clips, sometimes called binder clips or bulldog clips, have been a godsend when having to photocopy copious amounts of paper. They are robust, can securely hold loose sheets of paper and can also be used as bookmarks and cable tidies. When the metal handles are pressed against the paper, you can pile up papers easily. Alternatively, you can flip the handles up and hang on noticeboard pins in your notice board. For ease, I always carry my mini **foldable** scissors (for cutting off the plastic tape that surrounds the boxes containing reams of photocopying paper), and a few foldback clips around my lanyard, just in case I need to photocopy the odd sheet. When I am doing mass photocopying, I carry a small mesh bag containing my foldable clips.

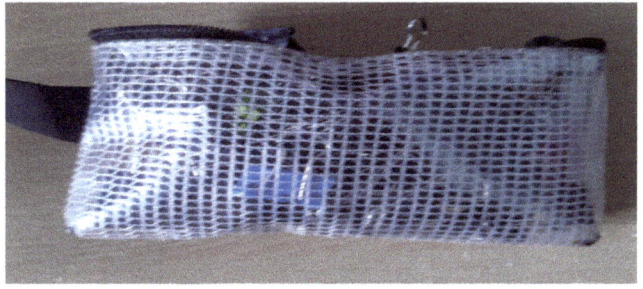

Picture 3: Foldback Clips

For bulkier amounts of paper, I use large foldback clips, but the 32mm clips fulfil general photocopying requirements. I buy mainly black clips, but I have some in different colours, which I use to separate worksheets according to differentiated levels of challenge; for example: red for SEND (Special Educational Needs and Disabilities), green for LA, yellow for MA and blue for HA. I don't need to use coloured clips often now because many schools are moving away from explicitly differentiated worksheets and prefer teachers to rely more on adaptive teaching methods; however, if differentiated resources are necessary and the layout of each sheet is very similar at first glance, I will group sheets together according to the colour of the foldback clips to prevent confusion. This is particularly useful when leaving cover work for supply teachers.

Although you could avoid confusion by photocopying different levels of challenge on different coloured paper or using different shapes (circles, triangles, squares), chillis (mild, hot, spicy) or stars directly on the sheet to reflect difficulty; for example: one star – easy; two stars – medium; three stars – challenging, but this is not a particularly sensitive way of differentiating. Also, coloured paper is more expensive and can create visual clutter in pupils' books. The foldback clips are an effective and simple solution for separating sheets. The only time I have used different coloured paper is for certain pupils with dyslexia who found it easier to read text on cream or light blue paper rather than white.

Another way in which I use binder clips is for coiling and clipping cables. Alternatively, if you prefer, Velcro strips can be used and there are even electronic accessories organiser bags that you can buy online or in shops to house USB leads and HDMI cables.

Revolutionary Remote Clicker

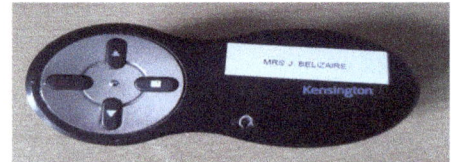

Picture 4: Clicker

Clickers (also called 'wireless presenters') have changed the way I move in the classroom. In the past, during the teacher-input stage of the lesson, I was generally fixed to the spot at the front of the classroom because I had to press the interactive board or keyboard arrow keys to present my presentation slides and, therefore, was unable to freely move around the classroom.

You don't want to make students seasick by constantly moving around the classroom, but being able to carefully circulate the classroom, supporting students with their learning and addressing any off-task behaviour makes teaching and learning so much easier.

For example, when I was recently helping one of my pupils during a maths lesson, I could refer to a previous slide with the click of a button on my remote without having to leave my pupil's side.

Using the clicker meant that we could have a conversation about the question displayed on the slideshow without me being metres away. The remote clicker I use also features a red laser pointer, which means I can focus on keywords within my slides; however, the laser does not show up very well on Clevertouch boards, but this may not be the case for all remote clickers. Important: Take care not to dazzle anyone with it, as it is a laser!

In addition, if you are presenting assemblies or professional development training, using a remote clicker means that you do not have to depend on anyone else to navigate the slides. My clicker does not have an integrated mouse feature but there are also some clickers with this feature included, if you prefer.

Sensational Storage

If you are lucky to have a filing cabinet already installed in your classroom, great! If not, the plastic storage unit is another essential organisation tool. There are other alternatives, such as concertina boxes, which you can carry around with you if you are not based in a specific classroom; however, for my needs, I find it easier to have deep drawer space. Below is a generic storage unit (emptied out) that I purchased, which has five deep drawers. It sits comfortably under my teacher desk without encroaching on my leg room when I am seated at the desk.

Picture 5: Storage Unit

Keeping your table surfaces clear sends the message of tidiness to your pupils, too; by modelling good habits, your students are much more likely to follow your lead. A main area of central storage is tidier than multiple receptacles dotted around everywhere as lots of boxes, in-trays, etc., just create more clutter.

I would have preferred a unit with six drawers and on wheels; however, the height of my teacher desk at school does not accommodate a taller unit. You will see from the labelled drawers, that maths and English each have their own drawer because they take place daily in the morning, whereas the afternoon lessons are further down. I also have laminates for each subject which I use every year. I find these laminates particularly useful if I ever need to leave cover work for supply teachers.

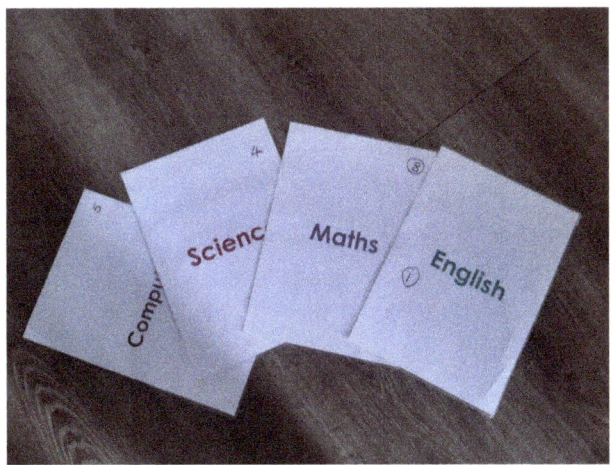

Picture 6: Subject Laminates

If you wish to further separate worksheets according to the days of the week, you could create laminates on different coloured paper according to days of the week to serve as dividers.

Picture 7: Weekly Laminates

If you don't have access to a laminator or time to make 'days of the week' laminates, you could use the wallets shown below to store your worksheets for each day of the week, according to the colours of the rainbow:

Picture 8: Colourful Wallets

I use the **'rainbow system'** for all kinds of things in my teaching; for example, the wallets above are what I use for my *White Rose* maths sheets – red is for Monday's work; orange is for Tuesday's work; yellow is for Wednesday's work and so on. These wallets can also be used as whiteboards as they are wipeable.

Jazzy Jackets

It is good practice to dress smartly in the workplace as it sets a professional tone. Without fail, I always wear suits or plain smart jackets with deep pockets as this is another practical way of storing key items requiring frequent access, such as my remote clicker and whiteboard pens. To add variety to my rather limited sartorial taste, I have a range of different coloured jackets featuring pockets that I can spread across a couple of weeks – my signature wear! I tend to steer away from heavily patterned jackets and prints so that I can team them up with a dress, black polo neck jumper or plain top. Donning a smart jacket every morning has truly reduced decision fatigue regarding what to wear for work. If jackets are not your thing, smart cardigans (not the sloppy, big-knit kind as these are too casual for school) work just as well. I always ensure that I plan what I am wearing the night before, so that I am not making decisions about what to wear in the morning.

If you truly want to simplify your wardrobe choices and create a uniform for yourself, you could do what Geri Horner does and wear one base colour (which in Geri Horner's case is white, which would not be practical in the classroom); however, if you have a particular colour preference or if your school has a strong colour brand that you want to adopt, this may be the best option for you.

Pupils do take notice of what you are wearing, and bright clothes are usually well received, but avoid busy patterns as these can be visually distracting, especially for pupils with autism.

Top Tip: Wear smart comfortable shoes because uncomfortable shoes will age you!

Advice on Avoiding Sartorial Slips

Check your school's dress code policy; for example, most schools do not like staff wearing denim or denim-like material, leggings, spaghetti straps or vests. Some schools expect male teachers to wear a shirt and tie and for women to ensure that their skirts are knee-length or longer. If in doubt, follow this advice that I once heard from a previous headteacher: "If you can see up it, down it or through it, don't wear it."

Lovely Lollipop Sticks

In the world of education, the humble lollipop has been used in multiple ways. You can buy class packs of lollipop sticks. Once you have a pack, write the name of each child onto an individual stick and place them in a pot/jar/bag. Here are some ways in which you could use them:

- Great for **pupil voice**, particularly in PSHE. Pull out a name without looking and elicit a response from the selected pupil. This is a super way of keeping pupils on their toes in an informal, relaxed way. If a pupil does not feel comfortable speaking in front of the class, you could ask them to write their response on a whiteboard whilst you quickly pick someone else. Sometimes, to engage pupils even more, I ask pupils to perform the job of pulling out names.

- When picking a **volunteer** for interactive games, lollipop sticks are a great way of keeping things random which, in pupils' minds, is fair.

- If you want to change or shake up **talking partners**, you could use lollipop sticks to pair pupils differently.

- I have assigned classroom monitors to help me keep my classroom spick and span but if you prefer not to have assigned classroom monitors, you could use lollipop sticks to choose pupils for **classroom jobs**.

Some teachers even make lollipop sticks a part of their **Transition Day** by handing each of their new-class-to-be a lollipop stick for them to customise as they see fit with felt-tip pens and sequins.

Marvellous Monitors

Children generally love to help with little jobs around the classroom and more hands make light work! I like to change the monitors every half-term for a range of jobs so that everyone has the opportunity to be of help at some point in the year. There are some beautiful bold name tags that serve this purpose that you can download from teaching sites, but the minimalist in me prefers a simpler idea. I use a laminated job list. Please see picture overleaf:

Monitors
Lunchboxes –
Exercise books –
Reading Logs –
ICT –
Bookshelf –
Funds –
*School Councillor

Picture 9: Monitor List

I write the names of those for each role in whiteboard pen, which I can rub out every half-term with ease. This is a more efficient use of my time as I don't have to spend time making and laminating individual labels, and it also takes up less room in the classroom.

Wonderful Whistle

Whistles are not only the preserve of specialist PE teachers; they can be used in other contexts, for example:

- Useful for **signalling a change of activity** in a discussion-based carousel when everyone is engrossed and a hand signal or the concierge bell won't work.
- When on duty, if there is no bell available, it is useful to have a whistle to **signal the end of playtime**.

- Always carry one on your person during school hours in the event of an emergency; for example, during a **fire drill** at a school I once worked in, the megaphone had been forgotten and my whistle was the only way in which to gain the attention of the entire school. It was just luck that I had it on me, as I had forgotten to remove it after my duty that day but since then, I have always worn one whilst on site.

Tremendous Thermos

I love my thermos flask because it is a source of comfort and calm. I like to place a slice of lemon or lime at the bottom and then pour hot water on top for a refreshing yet hot beverage. In the summer, I do the same but put the thermos in the fridge overnight and it keeps the drink cold throughout the day. When looking for a thermos, I suggest that you find one that has a handle, is dishwasher safe and has a stainless-steel inner casing, as stainless steel is durable, more hygienic than plastic and does not absorb odours.

Lovely Lunch Bag

Ensure that you purchase a well-insulated lunch bag to keep your lunch fresh. A well-sealed lunch bag also means that any accidental spills are well contained. I put an ice block in it to keep my lunch cold, so I do not have to label my lunch and leave it in a communal fridge.

Terrific Timer

Maximising learning time is important in the classroom. One of the ways in which this can be done is by using a basic electronic timer. The timer shown below was bought in *Asda* but other brands are available. It features a magnet on the back, which means it can be attached to the metal part of my flipboard chart frame so pupils can see it during timed tasks or tests. It also has a tripod feature, which means it is self-standing. You could use online timers as there are many fun ones available with stunning graphics, but why bother? Using a fancy online timer does not improve learning and my *Asda* timer is much easier, as I don't even need to switch on my computer.

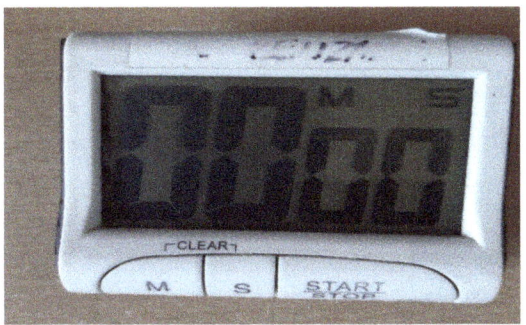

Picture 10: Electronic Timer

Using a timer also supports me with my time-management; for example, I find that if I am constantly watching the clock because I must be somewhere else at a certain time, I am not as focused on the task at hand as I should be – clock-watching, therefore, creates tension. Setting a timer to sound at a time of my choosing means that I don't have to keep clock-watching and can relax, fully engrossed in my work.

I have also used it when leading year group meetings to ensure that everyone is clearly aware when time is up. Despite time being a precious commodity to teachers, it is fair to say that some teachers are their own worst enemy and the ultimate time thieves. You will soon be able to recognise the worst culprits. I also use it for certain parents during Parents' Evenings; not all parents, just the ones I know might push the time limit.

It is also great for timing the class if there is chatter between lesson transitions. I don't say anything, I just hit the button and watch time accrue and usually this brings the class back to silence. I then write the amount of time wasted on the board. My pupils can redeem themselves if they behave impeccably after the 'loss-of-learning time infraction'; however, if there is little improvement, I continue to time them and will keep the pupils responsible for disrupting the class back. Of course, if a child is disrupting in a way that cannot be tolerated, follow the school's behaviour policy. In most schools, if a pupil is persistently being disruptive, you should have the option to send them to the **Senior Leadership Team (SLT)** or behaviour support.

Eggscellent Timers

Many schools provide egg timers, but I wanted a set of my own, so I bought a set of small egg timers from *Amazon*. For pupils who need sensory breaks or time outs, these are great. At the end of the day, I ensure that they are packed in bubble wrap and stored carefully.

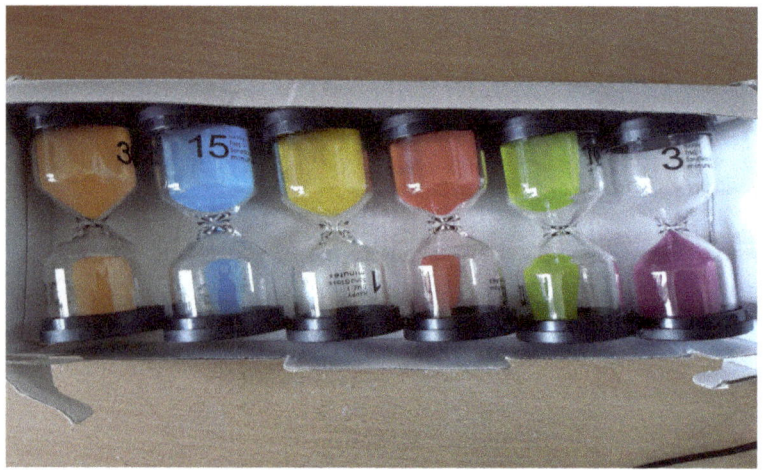

Picture 11: Egg timers

Versatile Visualiser

Hopefully, you will already have a visualiser installed in your classroom; however, this is not always the case. Two years ago, I bought a fantastic, portable *Okiocam* visualiser via *Amazon,* which has been well utilised in my lessons.

Here are some ways in which I have used my visualiser:
- Taken photographs of 'star' pupils' work to inspire them and others, as my visualiser has a photograph feature.

- Modelled and shared answers from a textbook so pupils can self- or peer-assess.
- Presented examples of children's work for whole-class feedback.
- Modelled art techniques à la Blue Peter.
- Demonstrated science experiments.
- Shown stitching techniques during textile lessons.

My visualiser is one of my staples and it is even small enough for me to carry in a pencil case.

Magnificent Magnifier

If you teach a child with a visual impairment, it is helpful to enlarge photocopies of task sheets (122% on A3) and use an easy-to-read, large font style in your teaching slides and worksheets; however, it is not always feasible to enlarge certain items because sometimes content is missed when enlarged to such an extent. It is in these instances that the magnifying globe is a real friend to a pupil with a visual impairment because it glides across paper smoothly, which means it does not have to be held in the hand like a magnifying glass and is compact enough to be stored in a tray.

Awesome Amplifier

Teaching is voice intensive and if your voice is on its last legs, you may wish to turn to a voice amplifier. This certainly helped me in one school where I felt extremely run-down, and my voice was wearing thin. If you need the attention of the whole school, for example, in the playground, then this is also useful if no megaphone is available (and it makes you feel a bit like a rockstar!)

Picture 12: Voice Amplifier

Transformational Tablet

Tablets are a regular fixture in classrooms nowadays for pupils to access resources such as *Times Tables Rockstars*, *Accelerated Reader*, and *Google Translate* for newly arrived EAL pupils, but I have used the tablet in other ways; for example, I taught a visually impaired pupil who, with her tablet, was able to mirror what was on the IWB (interactive whiteboard) during lesson. If the mirror facility failed, she would take a photograph of the teaching slides.

I also use tablets to take photographs of pupils' work, as I find the quality of photos on tablets much better than most classroom cameras or mobile phone cameras.

Calming Concierge Bell

In conjunction with hand signals, the concierge bell can be useful when pupils are engrossed in their work, and you want to get their attention without raising your voice. I like the sound of the concierge bell because it is gentle on the ear, but there are many other kinds of bells out there from which to choose.

Positive Post-its

Post-it notes are one of the best inventions, aren't they? I always have a pack of Post-it notes, both square and rectangular, within easy reach. Here is a quick low-down on how I use Post-it notes in the classroom:

- **Pupil voice** – During and at the end of English units, I seek feedback from my class about what went well (WWW) and even better if (EBI). You'll be amazed at how responsive and honest children are. Pupil voice is powerful when used appropriately and can inform my lesson planning, as it allows me to improve my practice in light of pupil comments; in fact, I warmly receive feedback from my students because it creates better learning experiences and enables me to grow every day as a teacher. Having a receptive mindset is vital for personal growth and your **CPD (Continuing Professional Development)**. For example, during an English unit on poetry, one pupil wrote that they felt they had learned so much about figurative language and wanted to do more. If I had my way, poetry would be taught as the first unit of the year in KS2 (Key Stage 2) because pupils quickly learn so many literary devices which they can then transfer to story writing. I have never understood why many schools still insist on narrative units at the beginning of the academic cycle because, to my mind, that is comparable to asking someone to walk or run before they've even learned to crawl! Anyway, that's a gripe for another book.

- **Positive Feedback** – Post-it notes are great for writing positive notes about the pupils whilst they are working; for example, if you can see that a pupil is working well, write it down on a Post-it note and leave it on their table. Of course, in addition to this, you may wish to provide them with house points, merits, postcards home or *Marvellous Me* messages, but the majority of pupils enjoy receiving a kind note from their teacher in live time, especially those who are self-conscious and do not like the limelight when praised verbally in front of the class.

- **Lessons** – Great for PSHE and Relationships and Sex Education (RSE); for example, during one of my RSE sessions,

I invited students to write any questions they had on a Post-it. This meant that I could decide which questions were age-appropriate and **maintain control** over the subject matter under discussion in the lesson instead of being caught off guard by X-rated random questions.

- **End-of-term Activities** – Post-it notes are often great for end-of-term games, such as 'Guess Who?' I would write keywords from the lesson on Post-it notes and then place them face down on students' desks. Without looking at the Post-it notes, students lightly placed the notes on their foreheads (make sure you check for any allergies on your medical register beforehand) and they had to then guess the keyword by asking a series of closed questions. You could also use this game at the end of the year for a multitude of topics, such as subject-specific vocabulary, figures of history, celebrities, songs, films, etc.

- **Voting** – At some point in every school, pupils will be invited to vote on something, usually School Council, Eco Warriors, etc. Whenever this occurs, I unleash Post-it notes. In a flash, I stick the Post-it notes on students' desks, and they write the name of the person they wish to be nominated for School Council and fold it a couple of times. This is far easier than cutting up individual tiny pieces of paper for pupils to write on.

- **Worry Box** – In my class, pupils can write their worries on a Post-it note and put it through the slot of our classroom worry box.

- **Notes** – If I ever need to leave a message on a colleague's desk, I will quickly write my message on a bright yellow Post-it note.

Welcoming Worry Box

I previously mentioned a 'Worry Box', and this can be purchased, or you could make one, if you have time. I made one by customising a box I found at home and covering it in a beautiful photograph from an expired calendar I had lying around. The children like it, and I check it at regular intervals.

Most children prefer to talk to their chosen adult(s) rather than writing down problems on a Post-it, but the class like the fact that it is there in case it is a particularly sensitive issue, or they don't want to talk within earshot of their peers. It is important for teachers to remember that they are not just teaching the children's brains, they are teaching the whole child and when pupils can see that their teacher cares about them as a person, it makes a difference to the pupils' wellbeing.

The Power of Plants

As a teacher, you will be in your classroom for several hours a day and it is important to make your environment homely and comfortable for yourself and your class. One of the ways in which I do this is through plants, as it is lovely to have some nature in the classroom. In my classroom, I have a Spider plant and a Snake plant (Sansevieria), which is the plant of choice for many offices as they are great for improving air quality. Furthermore, having plants in the classroom is also a great way of discussing biology and encouraging pupils to look after the plants. Plants also have the power to soothe; for example, once I encountered a very distressed child during lunchtime and managed to reduce his stress by kindly asking him to water my plants while talking to him; therefore, never underestimate the power of plants!

Home Is Where the Heart Is

I tend to use a minimalist approach when decorating my classroom, such as using the same-coloured backing paper for each display board to keep my work environment clean and simple. That said, a classroom is for children, too, so there needs to be a balance to avoid the classroom becoming too clinical. To create a homely yet educational feel, I bought an owl doorstop in a garden centre sale, and it now takes pride of place in the book corner of my classroom. I also brought in some cushions for the book corner area to make the seating area more inviting, and I also found an 'I Love Reading' image online, which I enlarged in colour on A3, and then had it laminated – it makes for a lovely poster and didn't require me dipping into my purse. If your budget stretches, you could even bring in some fresh flowers to brighten up the classroom once in a blue moon.

Super Shredder

In the past, rather than searching for the shredder in the school office (which, from experience, is often over-flowing or jammed), I had a small cross-cut shredder which I placed on my desk or on my shelf. I find it so much easier to shred items as I go along rather than bagging it all in a secure bag at the end of the year or having to traipse around the school looking for a functioning shredder.

That said, some schools are taking the shredding bin approach to avoid jammed machinery. This means that the items for shredding are emptied into confidential shredding bags at regular intervals; therefore, you may not need a personal shredder.

Powerful, Portable Whiteboard

A fantastic former teacher colleague of mine shared this nugget with me as she used it with her least fluent learners during Guided Writing sessions. She would scribe and generate ideas on the whiteboard with a small group, which could be left on the children's tables as a reference point for their own ideas. I purchased one of my own many years ago through *Amazon*. It is A3 in size, self-standing and has two sides – one is plain, and the other is squared.

Picture 13: A3 Whiteboard for Guided Sessions

Marvellous, Magic Whiteboard Paper

If your school does not have a flipchart stand with paper, an alternative is *Magic Whiteboard Paper,* as it is reusable.

Ultimate Upload - USB Passport or USB Sticks

Nowadays, if you're fortunate, your school will have different systems for backing up the work you carry out on the school computer, such as **OneDrive** or **Google Drive**. It is imperative that you back up your work regularly because you do not want all your hard work to vanish before your very eyes due to a malfunctioning computer. This happened to me once in a previous school; I tried to retrieve it myself and even contacted the IT services but to no avail. Needless to say, I never repeated this mistake again and have *Microsoft Word* set to 'Autosave' and back up frequently.

Whenever I start a new job, I make certain that anything private and confidential, such as SEND, pupil medical notes, assessment results, school logins, school-related admin and pupil-related admin (such as register lists, reports, school photographs, etc.), go into a separate folder named **'Private & Confidential'**. This means that if I need to copy my own teaching files and folders off-site, I do **not** inadvertently copy this folder.

All I want to do is ensure that my lesson planning and CPD certificates are backed up throughout the academic year. When I move to a different school, in the spirit of sharing good practice, I leave whatever resources I have made on the school system because as cheesy as it sounds, sharing is caring.

Speaking of sharing, I would like to highlight a beautiful act of kindness and generosity that was extended to me during my first primary teaching role. An outstanding teacher in the school where I was working at the time kindly transferred all her resources to me, and I have never forgotten it. She didn't have to do that; I never hinted or asked her. She wanted to, out of the goodness of her heart, as she knew that I was new to primary teaching. I learnt so much from her excellent planning and, if she should ever read this book, I would just like to say a massive thank you to her, as her kindness touched me then and continues to move me still. I have never understood teachers who are happy to take and take but keep their own resources and ideas close to their chest and never share. I am of the school of thought that if what I do benefits other classes, surely that's a good thing for children's learning. We limit ourselves and our students if we hide effective practice. When all teachers are passionate about their vocation and are 100% behind working collaboratively, it is a great experience for pupils and educators alike.

Furthermore, if you ever decide to move to another school, you will want to ensure that you have a copy of your files readily available on a separate device of your own so that you can re-use some of what you have created previously, instead of wasting valuable time reinventing the wheel every time you start a new role. For ease, I use a USB stick or USB passport (which is **password protected**) for copying lesson plans and my own personal *Google Drive* account. *Google Drive* is particularly useful in schools where USB/memory sticks are not permitted on-site, as this means that I can then transfer from *Google Drive* to a USB stick or USB passport in the comfort of my own home.

Other Useful Teaching Equipment

It is my hope that many of the items outlined beneath will be provided by the school in which you work. You can see from the table below that there is a great deal to consider when kitting out your classroom, but it is entirely up to you what you wish to include in your bag of teacher goodies; please feel free to cherry-pick. For example, not all schools will require a lunchtime laminate, radio, black socks, A3 pupil wallets or a calligraphy pen, as some schools will use coloured wrist bands for lunch options, whiteboard erasers instead of socks, and pencil cases instead of A3 zipper wallets.

Sometimes, being a teacher can feel like an exhausting military operation; however, being well organised really helps, especially when things do not go to plan, as you can often improvise successfully if you have useful materials in your teaching arsenal. You want your classroom to be a fully functioning command centre. Here is an itemised list in alphabetical order:

Address labels	Some schools word-process the learning objective (L.O.) and success criteria (S.C.) of the lesson on Avery labels so that students do not have to spend time in the lesson copying these. Another use for labels is name tags; for example, if an external visitor is teaching your class, it helps if the children have labels bearing their names to allow the visitor to refer to each child by name when eliciting responses, rather than having to point, and it helps the wheels of participation to run more smoothly.
	In addition, address labels are great for labelling pupils' stationery. I tend to cut the labels in strips before applying to pens and pencils.

Antibacterial hand gel	PPE is not always readily available now the height of COVID-19 appears to be behind us; however, I remain cautious and always have my own bottle of antibacterial hand gel with me, which I keep out of reach of children. I have one which I tie around the outside of my handbag.
Antibacterial spray	I recommend the aerosol Dettol Spray. It is great for spraying the classroom chairs and can be used on fabric, too. Make certain that you spray in a well-ventilated room and that you do not spray in the presence of your class in case they have asthma or some other respiratory condition. If I need to, I spray during lunch and after school.
A4 arch file	Although I strive to be paperless by planning electronically, you will need a file for behaviour incident forms, CPD documents, homework record checklist and reading record logs. In this arch file, I also insert any spare copies of resources so that I can share with absent pupils what they missed during their absence and better support them. I use dividers to separate the documents for ease of reference.
Art	These are some of the items I have in my art cupboard: • Coloured pencils • Felt-tips • Rainbow selection of poster paint • Water colours • A range of different brushes (thin, thick) • Palettes

	• Water containers (**Top Tip**: Never fill the containers right to the top; just fill at the half-way mark because if an accidental spillage occurs, there is less to clean up!) • Table covers • PVC glue • Charcoal • Oil pastels • Wax crayons • Old shirts for pupils to cover themselves in or, even better, art aprons • Child-friendly scissors If you work in a school with a dedicated area for art, none of the above will be needed which means less clutter in your classroom.
A3 document folder file zipper bag (extra thick)	These are also brilliant for keeping your pupils' stationery items, whiteboard and draft book neatly in one place. If your school has desks with integrated pupil trays, you can do away with these plastic bags altogether. I wish more schools would implement these desks because it means that pupils can neatly and quickly store their stationery. Also, it means that pupils don't have to disturb the class by asking to leave their seats to retrieve forgotten items.
Black socks	Socks to wipe students' mini whiteboards and hold their pens (if your school does not provide pencil cases). You could even instruct them to stitch their names on the socks as part of an introductory Design and Technology lesson.

Blu Tack	You'll need a few packs for the academic year. I use this to position how I want my corridor display to look before I permanently affix display content with a staple gun. For the working walls inside my classroom, I use Blu Tack or drawing pins so that I can easily change students' work on display, my posters and keyword cards.
Calculators	Useful for maths games where students need to check their partner's answers quickly. This is not equipment that you should have to purchase.
Classroom carpet	This is a great resource for Early Years. Carpets with a 6 x 5 array work well for large classes. I like the carpets with different coloured shapes, fruits, pebbles or animals, as this means children can easily remember their designated spot. These carpets range from £300 upwards; therefore, the school should provide them if you work from nursery to Key Stage 1.
Clipboard	Great for trips when you need to take a register and carry admin. Also, useful when typing copious amounts of text onto the computer as you can place it next to the side of your computer.
Coloured tabs (sticky index tabs page markers)	Index sticky notes are great for highlighting important information or feedback to pupils, as they instantly see the tab and know that there is a comment for them to respond to. You don't have to do this with all pupils as this would be rather time-consuming, just the ones who frequently fail to acknowledge teacher feedback. Once the pupil has acted on teacher feedback, they tick and initial the tab so that you can find it easily for review.

Command picture hanging strips	These are useful for hanging up frames. These hanging strips are damage-free and, when applied correctly, hold strong.
Cushions	I add a couple of basic cushions to the reading corner to make the area look more inviting.
Days of the week and months of the year display cards	Have these printed out in a sans serif font to help dyslexic pupils and print them on cream paper and laminate them. In general, I am trying to reduce lamination to be environmentally friendly, but I think you'll agree that if you're using them year in, year out, it's worth laminating them. Of course, if you want to model handwriting, you could do away with this altogether and write the date on your whiteboard by hand each day.
Dictionaries and thesauruses	These are like gold dust in some schools! If you're not blessed with a class set of dictionaries and thesauruses, it is a good idea to have a fully comprehensive dictionary at your disposal. Alternatively, pupils could use electronic dictionaries on tablets.
Door signage poster	The 'Door signage poster' is a quick and easy way of communicating with my class and staff before they enter my classroom. Here is the layout of what mine looks like: Where is **Mrs Belizaire**? • Come on in! • In a meeting • Study session with students • In another classroom • Be back soon

	• Gone for the day
	• Silent working due to assessment
	• Please do not disturb
	I place a maths counter (with Blu Tack on the back) on the bullet point next to my chosen option.
Door wedge	I bought a cheap plastic one from a pound shop many years ago and have it as a backup, as most schools provide door wedges. They are useful for ventilation purposes. **Important**: Make sure any door that you are wedging open is NOT a fire door.
Ear defenders	Very useful to have during music lessons. If you have a class of 30 children playing percussive instruments, it can be painful on the ear drums, especially if you cannot send groups of children to other rooms. I also ensure that I have ear defenders (supplied by the school) for certain pupils with autism.
	While on the topic of ear defenders, I have some small **ear plugs** that I use when marking books during lunch time to reduce extraneous noise. They help me to concentrate more effectively.
Electric pencil sharpener	Worth purchasing one of these as the plastic ones break easily and the blades of the metal ones get dull quickly.
Erasable Frixion pens	I buy these as I find them indispensable when marking English work. If I make a mistake when writing comments, I can quickly erase, and this means that I avoid crossings out in pupils' books (which never looks good) and can maintain and model high standards of presentation.

Fine-nibbed pens (1.0mm)	Great for those pesky forms which have little space in which to write.
First-aid box	Many schools have first-aid boxes dotted around the school. I have been fortunate to work in schools where first-aid boxes in classrooms and corridors (on high-level shelves) are standard. If your classroom does not have a first-aid kit, it would be worth requesting a school-approved one; these need to be maintained appropriately. **Top tip:** Have sick bags or a sick bowl to hand! I have learned this the hard way.
Flipchart and flipchart pens	You don't have to use the interactive screen all the time in lessons as the flipchart is a fantastic resource. Most schools provide their staff with a flipchart and pens but, if not, an alternative option is the Magic Whiteboard Paper I mentioned earlier.
Plastic foldable stool	I'm quite short and I find this handy when affixing items to the top of the main whiteboard.
Glue gun	Great for Design and Technology lessons and quick fixes that need doing, such as book spines.
Glue sticks	I spend some time teaching my pupils how to use glue sticks; otherwise, they are quickly wasted. I always have a pack that I buy myself as backup for the reasons outlined for pens.
Guillotine	I bought a small 'Amazons basic' guillotine from *Amazon* because school guillotines jam frequently. It is, therefore, useful to have one as a backup as I prefer to minimise worksheets to A5 to reduce photocopying costs and guillotine them because folded A4 concertina worksheets look messy. Where possible, I try to avoid gluing

	in worksheets and prefer to find other ways of involving pupils in their learning.
Hand lotion	If you're anything like me, you wash your hands a great deal throughout the day. Having hand lotion easily available on my desk means that I can moisturise my hands and stop dryness.
Highlighters	Most schools use some variation of RAG (traffic-light) to review students' books, such as pink for great understanding; orange/yellow for partial understanding; and green for not understood; schools should provide these for you. Highlighters are also useful for school events, such as trips or swimming lessons; for example, I use pink for pupils with no swimming and this makes it easy to see at a glance who has no swimwear. If you're a visual person like me then this use of colour coding is useful.
Hole puncher	Worth having one for documents that you don't want to place in plastic wallets. Hole punchers are also useful for lever and linkage lessons when using split pins in Design and Technology.
Insect repellent	Believe it or not, being bitten can be an occupational hazard. During one teaching stint, I resorted to spraying my legs with insect repellent because I kept being bitten. I never spotted any fleas or bed bugs, but the carpet always smelled musty despite being vacuumed on a regular basis; therefore, I concluded that they must have been some blood-thirsty bugs with a taste for me lurking in the carpets!
Italic calligraphy pens	These are not essential but are great for special occasions, such as writing pupils' certificates, birthday cards, etc.

Laminator	I have my own small laminator (I can't remember where I bought it) and pouches. During the summer break, I laminate at home for my display boards and work on my classroom during the summer holiday, as I find this less stressful than trying to do everything during INSET. It's a laminator that also doubles up as a guillotine.
Laminates for English and Maths	I find that exposing pupils to sentence types from the outset truly raises the level of pupils' written expression. If you key in 'Alan Peat Sentence Types' in your search engine, you will find many free resources. To save on lamination pouches and having to distribute another set of laminates, on the back of the English laminate, I place a times tables mat with the four operations and multiplication grid which I found on http://www.instantdisplay.co.uk/. Pupils just flip the laminate when necessary. For reasons of copyright, I am unable to share the image of it here.
Laptop riser	If you are heavily dependent on using a laptop at work, I would advise you to employ a laptop riser as it makes word-processing documents less of a strain on the wrists and fingers. Another option, which is cheaper, is to place your laptop on a sturdy A4 binder. Your school may already have a laptop riser as part of the teacher's desk.
Lap tray	If you find yourself during your PPA slot without a PPA room because of interviews or school meetings being held in the PPA room, you can hunker down with your lap tray and books in your car (if you drive to work) or work on a lap tray in a room without tables. I have

	done this in previous schools because the only other room that was always available was the staffroom, but I never found this a productive environment in which to work because I ended up engaging with or being interrupted by colleagues!
Large lockable safety box	Jewellery should not be worn by pupils during PE days; however, there is always one! In such cases, it is a good idea to have a large lockable safety box as it keeps valuables safe and deters theft.
Large transparent pencil case	I used to use a lovely tin for all my marking paraphernalia, as it was a gift from one of my former pupils and I wanted to use it but found that I spent more time rummaging through it than marking! Now, I just use a large pencil case which allows me to see what I need immediately, due to it being transparent. I use the tin as a compartment for my drawer.
Lunch choices poster (laminated)	This is a laminated A3 poster that you can re-use each day. To avoid pupils asking me individually what the lunch choices are, I place a plastic knife and fork around my poster to make it obvious what the poster relates to. This is an example of how I presented my poster: **Today's Lunch Choices** 1. Meat option _____ 2. Vegetarian option _____ 3. Alternative option _____ (such as tomato pasta and jacket potato) 4. Dessert option _____

	Some schools use colours as opposed to numbers or distribute wrist bands, but this layout can be easily adapted. If you work in a school where individual choices are pre-ordered online, then none of the above is necessary.
Magnetic buttons	Many whiteboards in schools are magnetic; therefore, magnetic buttons can be used as a quick alternative to Blu Tack to hold up sheets, notices, vocabulary lists, etc., at the front of the class. My magnetic buttons were included with the whiteboard I bought but you can also source them.
Magnetic whiteboard erasers	Great for keeping on top of wiping your whiteboard. I sometimes use mine to double up as a magnetic button.
Marking bag	For light marking, it is good idea to have a 'bag for life' in your stockroom cupboard, as you won't want to necessarily lug a suitcase or crate on wheels for a set of books that could easily be carried in a bag.
Maths equipment Picture 14: Maths Manipulatives	Recently, I purchased this for 1:1 and small group work. In my current classroom, the school provides a set of maths manipulatives with each tray containing the following: • MathLink Cubes • 100 bead strings • Dice • Counters • Plastic Place Value Sliders (great for LA/SEND) • Rulers

Mini hoover or dustpan and brush	I am extremely fortunate that my pupils love tidying up and share my love of keeping our classroom tidy. I have a simple dustpan and brush, but one of my former colleagues had a mini battery powered hoover which his students absolutely loved; therefore, I might splurge and purchase one of my own for the next academic year.
Miniature wooden pegs	Great for working walls and hanging up text maps.
Nail scissors	It is worth purchasing some nail scissors as these are very useful when cutting out the fiddly sections of individual letters for display boards.
No entry sign	Most pupils would never dream of entering a teacher's stockroom cupboard; however, it doesn't hurt to signpost certain areas as strictly off limits because it removes any doubt by making your message clear. I place this on the front of the cupboard door which stores the more expensive items I have purchased, such as: my suitcase (I'll explain later), guillotine, voice amplifier and visualiser (when not in use). I bought my no entry sign online, but you could easily make one by copying an online image and laminating.
Paper	In case of exercise book shortages, ensure that you always have some plain paper, lined paper and squared paper in your classroom.
Paper weight	I have two beautiful glass paperweights that I use but they come with a warning: Don't leave them directly in sunlight as I heard a horror story about someone who left their paperweight in direct sunlight and then their window netting caught fire.

Pavement chalk	I have used pavement chalk to great effect in some maths lessons. Once the pupils had mastered the basics, I took them outside to perform mathematical calculations in groups on the pavement. The children did not have to think about space as there was plenty, and being outside put them at ease. Having ample space to write also motivated them to show their workings in full.
PE box	It is useful to keep a few bean bags, skipping ropes and cones, in case you must do PE in a venue with no PE equipment whatsoever! Yes, this has happened to me; however, I am thankful for this experience as I have never been caught out since. I also have laminated activity cards which serve as keep-fit stations and require very little equipment.
Pens	Children go through handwriting pens like they are going out of fashion! In addition to supplies from school, I also buy a pack of my own because schools tend to run out of pens at some point in the year and it sometimes takes a while for orders to come in. I have found Berol pens to be reliable but there are other decent brands available. Whatever you do, don't buy cheap pens as it's false economy because they rarely last and sometimes leak.
Photocopier access	Make certain that you obtain a photocopier number or card as soon as possible. If you receive a photocopying card, guard it well!

Picture frames (A4)	Most teachers have a noticeboard area for themselves. To keep my teacher wall space as uncluttered as possible, I minimise a photocopy of my timetable to fit into a cheap, simple white A4 frame. I do this to support any cover staff who might need to know what the year group's timetable looks like in the event of unplanned absence. I apply this to the wall, using *Command Picture Hanging Strips*.
Protractors	If you're teaching UKS2, you will need enough for each pupil.
Radio	I have always had a small radio in my classroom because during lunchtime, I sometimes like to listen to music. If I have had a particularly trying day, I listen to classical music or some spa-like music on *YouTube*. If you have access to *BBC* Sounds on your classroom computer, you could dispense with a radio altogether and free up space in your classroom.
Raffle tickets	I have not always used this system but with some of my more challenging classes, I used raffle tickets to encourage acts of great citizenship, such as kindness, helpfulness and teamwork. I would write the name of the pupil who demonstrated good citizenship on the back of the raffle ticket and then the pupil would place it in my golden raffle box. Each week, a raffle would be drawn, and the winner received an item of stationery or a reading book.
Rubber bands	Great for wrapping around books, if you need to separate them out into groups for intervention, etc.

Storage boxes	I bought three faux wicker storage cubes many years ago and they are still going strong. I use these to store miscellaneous items in my stockroom cupboard, as some stockrooms may not have a great deal of shelving space.
Spring-loaded scissors	It is well worth having a pair of spring-loaded scissors or high-quality large scissors which you can use for cutting large swathes of paper for display purposes. Spring-loaded scissors are easier on the hands but ensure that you keep them out of reach of children.
Spare lids	Remember to keep the lids from expired pens and glue sticks as lids always go missing.
Spray bottle	Spritz yourself! During extreme temperatures, it is good to have an empty spray bottle available that you can fill with water and then spray yourself to keep yourself cool. The children also love spraying themselves in hot weather. It is worth keeping a clean empty bottle in your stockroom cupboard for those potentially sizzling summers.
Spare equipment tray	If you are lucky enough to have some spare pupil trays, you could stock them up with a handful of stationery items as this will allow pupils to be self-sufficient when sourcing writing equipment. If not, an old biscuit tin should do the trick.
Stamps and stickers *Picture 15: Stamps*	Here is a collection of stamps that I have personally collected over the years. The stamps are: • Next steps • Show your working out • Supply Teacher • Improve your presentation

	• Please finish work • Excellent • Merit • Good Children of all ages love seeing a star in their books. Stickers are great source of motivation, too. The supply stamp is useful because not all supply teachers mark or stamp work; therefore, you could use this stamp to distinguish between lessons conducted by supply and yourself. This makes it clear to pupils, parents and SLT which lessons were taught by whom.
Stapler and paperclips	Staplers are useful to have for when the photocopying machine runs out of staples when you're collating work. Make certain that you label your display staple gun with your classroom name; otherwise, it tends to go walkies! When using a display board stapler, a great tip is to staple at an angle on the board so that the staples are not fully depressed into the display board. This makes the removal of staples, when changing or taking down old displays, a piece of cake. Paperclips are useful for the distribution of card games and general collation.
Strong plastic wallets (A4)	I am trying to reduce my plastic consumption and prefer to hole punch. I used to have multiple colour-coded A4 arch binders sitting on my shelf filled with documents in plastic wallets but not now, as I strive to be paperless and store most materials electronically. Sometimes, wallets are necessary for protecting key documents, such as CPD certificates. Make certain that you buy

	strong plastic wallets as the thin cheap ones are false economy.
Strong plastic box for children's water bottles	Useful to keep all the bottles in one place and, in the event of leaks, the spillages are contained. Spare pupil equipment trays also work just as well.
Small suitcase	I use it for carrying books to the PPA room so I can mark. It has several pockets, has great depth, is on wheels and I can lock it with a padlock. I have also used it when moving school or classroom as I can fill it up with many items. I would also like to make the point that when I leave a school or classroom, it does not take me long to gather my belongings because **I am almost paperless and discard items as I go along. I don't hold onto items that hold no value.**
'Thank you' cards	I always keep a pack of 'thank you' cards because I like to show my appreciation to pupils and parents when they provide cards and gifts. I prefer to write the cards up on the day whilst thanking them is still fresh in my mind, rather than handing out the cards later.
Thick cardigan/ poncho	School halls are nearly always cold and draughty. It is worth having a long, thick cardigan or smart overcoat. I have a smart poncho which works just as well.
Tipp-Ex	Useful for redacting worksheets before photocopying pages from books or ready-made worksheets.

Tissues	Again, I always carry a pack of pocket tissues in the event that anyone has a sneezing fit, a heavy cold or starts crying, but your school should provide a box of tissues for your classroom.
Tripod pens for pupils with handwriting difficulties	I purchased a pack of 10 as I had a pupil who struggled with his handwriting and found these useful. There are also tripod grips available which work in the same way. You can place these tripod grips around writing equipment like a sheathe.
Visual timetable	For bordered paper, display lettering and visual timetables, you can reduce your workload by downloading materials from well-known teacher sites, such as *Twinkl*. If you do not have access to such sites, you can make your own by searching online for relevant images. Alternatively, if you want to personalise your visual timetable, you could use an app, such as *Bitmoji or Apple's version, Memoji*. If you make your own subject cards, it will take some time but once laminated, they can be used year after year. For ease, you can add a strip of Velcro to the area where you wish to display your visual timetable and then place small Velcro squares to each subject card. Alternatively, Blu Tack or magnets could be used. **Top Tip**: Ensure that you organise the subject cards alphabetically to avoid time wastage. I wrap two elastic bands, criss-cross style so I can easily flip through the subject cards without them spilling out.

Wavy scissors	Easy way of framing pupils' work for display. This is something you can do now and then as it can be a bit time-consuming.
Wet wipes	Great for cleaning surfaces; for example, whenever I work in a shared space, I still insist on cleaning the desk area before setting down to work.

Wet wipes are great for cleaning paint off tables during art lessons, too. Also, at the end of the year when pupils' trays are being emptied for the new class, I provide wet wipes so pupils can clean the inside of their trays. |
| Whiteboards | You should not have to source these as most schools have them. Very useful in the classroom for instant feedback, quizzes, plenaries, etc.

I even carry my own whiteboard when supporting children 1:1 with their work, such as spelling out words, generating word banks, mathematical explanations, etc. |

The table above is exhaustive, but remember, many of the items in the table will already be provided by your school; therefore, you should not have to go to any extra expense or go on a special mission to search for these educational resources. You will just need to organise them tidily. By being aware of items that are integral to an effective classroom from the get-go, you won't be overwhelmed and will be better able to pace yourself throughout the year. Hopefully, this chapter has taken away the pain of having to think from scratch about the necessary equipment and has provided you with detailed, first-hand information about what is useful to have in a primary classroom.

In a nutshell

1. **Investing** in some key equipment will help you to feel more confident, organised and enable you to make better use of

your time. After all, a tidy, well-equipped classroom equals a tidy mind!

2. Keeping things **simple** and **organised** from the outset minimises time wastage and **boosts** your **brain power** and **energy levels**. Ensure that everything has a place!

3. Having **effective equipment** in place sets you up for success in the classroom.

A Teacher's Treasure Trove: Tools of the Trade

Notes

Chapter 2

Searching for Teaching Jobs and Spotting Red Flags

It is a sad fact that many teachers are leaving the teaching profession in droves due to various issues; namely, **poor pupil behaviour**, **burn out**, **workload** and **toxic work environments**. If you had to choose only one chapter to read from this book, I would urge you to select this one, as I want you to find a school that is right for you. You'll need to consider the type of school you wish to work in; for example, would you prefer a village school with mixed-year classes, a junior school, a primary school or a large academy? The prime function of this chapter is to put you in the picture and show you how to perform a 'deep dive' (to borrow one of Ofsted's most unlovable terms) into schools of interest. This chapter will spark curiosity about the schools in which you have expressed an interest and provide you with the tools to forensically profile a school. Searching for a teaching role requires putting your nose to the grindstone, but it's worth it. Your solid pre-application background check will also serve as a good basis for the interview process, should you decide to apply for the vacancy advertised and are short-listed for interview. Chronologically thinking, this chapter should have been the first chapter, but it is not the most upbeat of chapters and I did not want to instil fear or sour the tone of this book and frighten teachers away from the profession in the first instance. Hopefully, I haven't already scared you off here and you will still wish to read on and continue your teaching career.

Changing States of Schools

You can land a job in a great school and then find that it deteriorates with the passing of time because schools, by their very nature, are not static due to the changes in educational practices and human dynamics involved. For example, a new headteacher has the power to change the culture of a school and this can either be a blessing or a curse, depending on their personality and leadership style.

If you think a 'good' or 'outstanding' Ofsted report means that the school will be in excellent shape, don't count on it, as these inspections are merely snapshots in time and there is a growing movement of Ofsted detractors who strongly believe that Ofsted is no longer fit for purpose.

Conversely, not all schools with a negative inspection report are poorly performing schools. I worked in a school that was excellent, despite its 'Requires Improvement' grade and then, in its subsequent inspection, it received 'Good with Outstanding Features'.

Since September 2024, there have been adjustments to the Ofsted Inspection with the major change being the removal of the grade for overall effectiveness from graded inspections; however, I believe that this will do little to minimise the fear Ofsted instils.

Unfortunately, there are some schools that you truly do need to steer well away from. I don't think anyone has **mastered** the art of finding the ideal teaching role, and you cannot leave any stone unturned when visiting and investigating schools, but I do hope that this chapter helps you to **read between the lines** and **spot red flags**.

Looking for your ideal school is the time to sweat the small stuff! Paying close attention to your instincts is also vitally important. I promise you that you will rue the day when you ignore your gut instincts. **Please remember that opinions are my own.**

Online Presence

- Firstly, check out the school's website and use company review sites such as *Indeed* to see what both former and current staff have said about working in the school concerned (please note that not all schools will appear on *Google* or company review sites). Not all opinions on the websites are balanced but it's worth looking to weigh up the positives and negatives, just as if you were looking at *Checkatrade*, Trip *Advisor* or *Trust Pilot* for a holiday or hotel booking.

- Does the job advert only state **MPS** in the pay scale section and the phrase 'suitable for **ECTs (Early Career Teachers)**' or 'ECTs encouraged/welcome to apply'? If so, experienced teachers should consider whether it is worth applying, as it is highly likely that the school is seeking **ECTs** to reduce staffing costs. The current economic climate has led to these advert descriptions appearing more frequently in schools, apart from inadequate schools that are not permitted to take on ECTs until they are deemed fit to do so.

- How far are you willing to **travel** to work? What is your **mileage or commuter time radius**?

- What is your **Key Stage** preference?

Pay attention to the staffing list, governance, quality of pupils' work, curriculum maps/plans, tweets and *Facebook* page. **A note of caution:** *Twitter* (or *X*, as it is now known) and *Facebook* are PR machines but it's worth looking to see how the school brands itself. If the staffing list *only* features the leadership team, this is highly likely to be a **red flag**. I have only ever seen this twice and, in both cases, the schools were facing recruitment and retention issues. Other important features to examine are **governor meeting minutes, behaviour policy, marking policy, SEND provision,** and **newsletters** if readily available. I have included the 'Marking Policy' as an area to look at because it gives some indication of **workload**; for example, if the school uses one colour for marking, promotes the use of **secretarial codes** and peer- and self-marking as opposed to the teacher being expected to use three different colours for marking and write lengthy 'next step' feedback, then it is likely that the school has taken some steps to carefully consider how to reduce workload.

The **governor meeting minutes** can provide a wealth of information in a concise way as they sometimes feature details about the school's finances, complaints and upcoming events. You also get a feel for the tone of the school and how the governors hold school leaders to account. Is there transparency? Is robust questioning evident? Do governors reveal the strengths and weaknesses of the school, or do they gloss over problems and show that everything is hunky dory? I once had the pleasure of working with an excellent Chair of Governors who was not afraid to challenge the Senior Leadership Team. He had a wealth of educational experience – headship, Ofsted inspector – and the school was fortunate to have him. You ideally want to work in a school that shows candour in its school matters and is truly seeking to improve educational experiences for its students. Schools which are artificially rosy in their self-reporting about where they are on their journey to improvement, etc., are not likely to be good environments in which to work, due to the lack of rigour in terms of management.

- It is amazing how much you can glean about the culture and characteristics of a school through the **power of the written word**. How does the headteacher come across in writing? Are they conversational in tone? Do they sound warm, funny, empathetic yet professional, or are they cold and clinical? Does the headteacher have a great deal to write about, or are newsletters short and reliant on excerpts from other teachers? If the headteacher is not writing a great deal of content for whole-school newsletters, it could mean that the rest of the staff are required to double up as regular 'bloggers' in their own time.

- Do the newsletters inform parents about **staffing updates and keep parents fully apprised of the comings**

and goings of staff? Do the newsletters celebrate the achievements of both pupils and staff? If the headteacher fails to notify families about staffing news, such as staff departures, this might suggest that the headteacher does not value his/her workforce and is attempting to conceal retention issues.

- Does the school have an up-to-date **prospectus**? Is there **clarity of vision?** Is the school's **mission statement** precise, memorable and clear to the layman?

- Does the school have a **virtual tour video** on its website? If so, look. Does the video feature pupils talking? How do they appear? Do they look genuinely happy? What's the demeanour of staff like? Does the school appear to be self-satisfied and in love with its own slick branding ('style over substance' schools)? Is the headteacher self-promoting in tone, using 'I' a great deal instead of 'we'? It is very telling when headteachers use 'I' repeatedly in the context of school, as it suggests that they are not fully present for the school community, and it may also suggest that they could be the kind of headteacher who makes high-handed decisions. Could you see yourself working alongside the current school team based on the footage?

- What does the school look like? In one school video that I viewed, I was immediately put off applying due to the **layout** of the school, as it was too open plan for my tastes. Also, if I see a school with a therapy dog, I'm not interested. This isn't because I have anything against dogs – I love animals and nature and know how beneficial therapy dogs are – it's just that I am wary of dogs. Furthermore, with the prevalence of allergies, I am not sure it's wise to have permanent furry friends in schools. I hear the clamour of 'Bah humbug!' here.

- Is there a **school development** plan available? If accessible, is it precise, manageable and realistic?

- What are the school **roll numbers**? Some schools, such as village schools, tend to have small numbers on roll; however, schools within large towns or cities with low numbers, especially dwindling numbers, is often a warning sign that the school is in decline, and not held in high esteem by locals, or birth rates are low due to an ageing community. A school that is oversubscribed is generally a good indicator that the school is popular, well respected by the community and is likely to be well-resourced.

- How is the **school performing nationally**? What is the percentage of children achieving age-related expectations and greater depth? Do you enjoy the challenge of working in schools where significant educational improvement is needed? Check performance data tables on the government weblink: www.gov.uk/school-performance-tables.

- What is the proportion of **free school meals**, which is regarded as a metric of poverty? Go to the government link: www.get-information-schools.service.gov.uk. This will give you some idea about the catchment area. I have taught in disadvantaged areas and found working in these regions to be some of the most rewarding and fulfilling years of my teaching career, but working in schools situated in deprived areas is not for everyone, and such schools need strong leadership and effective behaviour systems, as the intake in these areas can be challenging. You need to find a school that suits you; otherwise, you run the risk of setting yourself up to fail. In general, teachers need copious amounts of grit and resilience, but in a challenging school, you need even more.

- What are the **class letters** addressed to parents like? Are they fawning in tone? Do **parents** come across as the bane of the school or are they greeted as friends who are supportive, engaged and loyal? Is there a **PTA (Parent Teacher Association)** or parent group affiliated to the school that raises funds or organises events for the children? In a school which is not well-resourced, PTAs are particularly helpful.

- Another tip, which I have only started doing in recent years, is to see if the school has appeared in the **news** by entering the name of the school along with the word 'newspaper' into a search engine. Often, the school will be in the news for positive things, such as charity work, celebrating a recent Ofsted report or competitions but, sometimes, some of what you discover about schools in both local and national media outlets can be eye-opening and jaw-dropping. At one school I visited, I immediately felt that the school was not a good fit for me. I could not precisely say why, as ostensibly it was a good school, I just had an odd feeling, a gut instinct, that I couldn't shake off. However, I didn't want to rule out the school completely as it had a great deal going for it, so I decided to do a bit of online digging by using the power of *Google*. It did not take me long to find a recent newspaper article online about the school. The establishment had been involved in a recent employment tribunal and, unfortunately, the school did not fare well.

Headteachers

- Does the headteacher have a **LinkedIn** or **Twitter (X)** feed? Does what they have to say align with your values and educational practice?
- When meeting the headteacher on the school tour, how does the headteacher come across? Do you think you could work together? Do you think that they have a pleasant personality? Do they seem genuine, or do they have an affected manner? Do they come across as having certainty and clarity of purpose? Does the headteacher cover lessons, do duties or teach regularly? This shows that they are willing to roll up their sleeves and work hard at the chalkface. If you like the school and reach the interview stage, do ask them what their leadership style is like and what they like most about working at their school.

- Some headteachers have more than one leadership style, or a style that combines the best elements of the key leadership styles. There are several leadership styles; namely: **instructional** (coaching and student outcome-based), **transformational** (vision-based, motivational), **constructivist** (development of learning), **servant** (focuses on the needs of others), and **strategic** (long-term goals informed by robust data and collaboration with stakeholders). Much more could be written here about leadership styles but for now I have distilled it for you. If the headteacher cannot articulate their leadership identity, then this might mean that they have not yet developed a clear and compelling vision of themselves as a leader, and this would set off alarm bells for me.

- Do you get the impression that the **headteacher is visible** within their school or do they lead from the office? One way in which to do this is to watch the headteacher's interactions with staff and the pupils during the school tour. Does the headteacher warmly greet staff and children by name when passing them in the corridors?

- Are any of the SLT or other staff featuring in CPD online videos, blogs or *Twitter (X)*? Some schools, particularly Multi-Academy Trusts (MATs) have their own *YouTube* channels where they post their CPD presentations online, some of which you can watch for free without registering; this will give you an idea of what is happening in the schools.

SEND Provision

What is the quality of **SEND** provision like? Is there a space(s) dedicated to intervention work? Are students receiving regular support? Does the school welcome specialists? I've been fortunate to have worked with a Local Educational Authority autism specialist who was incredibly helpful in my SEND development.

Is SEND CPD a high priority? In recent years, particularly since the height of the COVID-19 pandemic, it has been reported that SEND-related complaints from parents have soared dramatically. The government published in 2024 the following: "The number of pupils with an EHC plan *has increased* by 11.6% between 2023 and 2024 to 434,000, and by a total of 83.4% *since* 2016." You want a school that has an effective SENCO and TAs who understand the field of SEND. I have had the pleasure of working with brilliant SENCOs and TAs from whom I learned so much. They helped me to become a better teacher and, in doing so, enabled me to address the needs of my pupils. They suggested ideas for differentiation, helped with displays, marking and behaviour management. They also supported with the process of shared writing during English and conducted interventions, and one-to-one reading with pupils.

Many schools have had to cut costs and, sadly, this has often meant TA redundancies. Do look on the school website to see if classes have a TA attached. Although you can effectively teach *certain* classes without a TA, such as a class that is well-behaved and academically able. Generally, you will (at some point in your career) teach classes which will require more than making reasonable adjustments; for example, teaching Year 5 pupils working at Reception/Year 1 expectations. Teaching such classes without a TA is not easy. If the school in which you are interested has a TA attached to each class, this is certainly a tick for me.

Data and Ofsted

- What are the **SATs** (Standard Assessment Tests) results like? Is there an upward trend, plateauing or regression? Do take into consideration the impact of the pandemic when looking at the data. For me, data is not the be all and end all, but it's worth reading.

- Read the **Ofsted** reports thoroughly and take note of the dates because a great deal can happen in the years between inspections; you can't always believe the Ofsted badge. It is worth looking at the name of the headteacher listed on the Ofsted reports; for example, if the current headteacher of the school successfully took the school through consecutive inspections to the present day, then it is likely that the headteacher is effective. Furthermore, if job vacancies are rarely advertised in the school, this suggests that staffing is stable, and retention is good because morale is high. To know this, you will need to touch base with teaching advertising sites over time.

- On the other side of the coin, if you are open to working in a school which has been graded as 'Requires Improvement', I strongly advise you to diplomatically ask leaders how the school is improving or has addressed its weaknesses. If the member of SLT does not answer satisfactorily or appears prickly when asked, then perhaps the school is not the place for you. Schools rated 'inadequate' are not allowed to employ ECTs. If a school has received consecutively poor Ofsted reports, they are likely to become academies. If such schools close and re-open as an academy, they can recruit ECTs. Tread carefully if you have seen an advert for a school that has recently become an academy. Sometimes schools become academies because it works for them and has nothing to do with a poor Ofsted report, but do a background check using the Ofsted website on www.gov.uk/find-ofsted-inspection-report.

- In addition, make certain that you check the Parent View section of Ofsted. Sometimes the number of parents who engage with this survey is low, but this is not necessarily negative, as some parents may be too busy or feel that they're satisfied and have no inclination to report on the school in an official capacity.

- Keep your discerning ears to the ground; sometimes what you hear via word of mouth from teachers within the community can be valid and highlight ongoing issues.

Touring the School

Are there **multiple job ads** within the same school? Unless it is a brand-new school, this is cause for concern as it suggests a mass exodus and an ever-changing cast of staff. Poor staff retention is often related to systemic deficiencies. Of course, sometimes staff leave for other reasons, such as promotion, retirement, change of career and personal circumstances but when this is the case, it is often specified in the adverts. Furthermore, be aware of adverts which require '**resilience**' and '**strong behaviour management**' as these are likely to be behaviourally difficult schools; in fact, I would go a step further and substitute the word 'resilience' for 'sustained stress'. I also do not entertain school websites which are wordy and pepper their web content with the latest buzz words, as these schools are clearly not considering their main audience: parents and children.

If you are interested in applying for a job, you may wish to **visit** the school before applying. If you've seen a video of the school and did not like the layout of the school, then I would not bother visiting. If you do decide to visit, make certain that you **dress smartly** and wear **smart, comfortable shoes**; in fact, I always wear comfortable shoes in teaching because you're nearly always on your feet. Observe the environment around the school. Are there wide-open spaces or is it more of a concrete jungle? In some circumstances, you must decide whether you're a town mouse or a country mouse or both.

Does the school look visibly clean or are there mounds of rubbish in the playground? Do the staff and pupils look well-turned out? Is there a sink in each classroom? During the height of COVID, I was so thankful to have a sink with running water in my classroom. Are there enough toilets for staff within the block or vicinity where you'll be teaching? A strange question, you may think, but I have worked in a school where I had to go to another block to use the facilities.

Bear in mind that when you visit a school, you will be closely observed, and the school tour is often informally considered to be step one of the recruitment process. Make certain that you are smartly dressed and that you are prepared, as you may be asked interview-type questions during the school tour. If you don't want to be subjected to this type of pre-application scrutiny and decide against visiting schools or are unable to visit due to prior commitments, I would suggest that you search for school videos or *Twitter (X)* feeds to see the school in action.

If you spot friendly faces in the vicinity, pluck up the courage to speak to **locals**. On one occasion, when I was a very young teacher, I asked a passer-by if she was from the area and her take on the school I was visiting. What you are told may not be the gospel truth, but you can never have too much information when searching for your ideal school. You almost have to look at visiting a school in a similar way to the approach you might take when buying a house. In other words, be eagle-eyed!

Take note of the **demeanour** of staff when you visit? How did the reception staff greet you? What is the interaction and engagement between members of staff like? Do they look happy or harassed? Are they warm, friendly or cold and cliquey? Are staff in the staff lounge, enjoying a cuppa undisturbed during breaks? Non-verbal communication speaks volumes. **Do the pupils hold doors open, or do they push past you in haste, barely acknowledging you?** Do the pupils and staff smile or acknowledge you? Is there mutual respect and courtesy between children and adults?

I visited a school years ago where many staff strangely did not want to make eye contact with me (thankfully, this is rare) and I also sensed some professional tension between the headteacher and teachers when he showed me around. I did not put pen to paper to apply. Here are some **key questions** to consider:

- What's the **atmosphere** like? How do you feel as you walk around the school. Is it calm and harmonious? Do staff appear to have time for a snack at break with colleagues or is it breathtakingly frantic with staff moving at top speed?

- How many **photocopiers** are there that you can see? I would not be happy to work in a large school with only one photocopier! What do the exercise and textbooks look like? Are the **exercise books** well looked after or dog-eared and strewn with graffiti? Is there a lack of uniformity, in terms of presentation and content? Is there is a wide discrepancy between year groups and classes? If so, this could indicate a lack of organisational culture. During the height of COVID-19, school visits were limited, which made looking at pupils' work difficult. However, looking at pupils' work on the school website, usually labelled 'Student Gallery', can shed some light on work expectations, even if only the best samples have been uploaded for display.

- Are there **visualisers** in every classroom? Are there telephones or walkie-talkies in classrooms? I appreciate schools which provide immediate means of access to support; it's much better from a Health and Safety perspective.

- Are the **interactive whiteboards** in good working order?

- Are there **in-situ** computers in every classroom? Some schools expect staff to use the same laptop for the classroom and their teaching work at home. In-situ computers are generally sturdier, and they also mean that you need never worry about forgetting your laptop; however, this is not a deal-breaker for me.

- If you truly like the school from the get-go, don't be shy! If the opportunity presents itself, engage with staff who you see and ask how long they have been there? Is there a mix of **ages, experience and cultures**? Personally, I have learned so much from both new and veteran teachers; however, I would advise against choosing to work in a school with predominantly inexperienced teachers, as you may not benefit from the rich experiences of experienced teachers.

It's good if you can work in a school with staff from diverse teaching backgrounds.

- What does the **building** look like from the outside and inside? Are there many windows in each classroom? **Do the windows open?** I once worked in a classroom that only had one functioning window; this never bothered me until COVID arrived.

- Is there a dedicated **PPA (Planning, Preparation and Assessment)** room? Working in the staffroom is not a suitable environment for PPA. Some modern buildings don't have the nooks and crannies that old school buildings have. You don't want to have to lug books around during PPA or wet break/dinner, desperately trying to find a quiet space to work, as this is not conducive to focused working. If your school allows you to work from home, even better! I currently work in a school which allows me to have my PPA at home. This may not work for everyone but, for me, I get so much work done because I wake up early (06:30) and have no interruptions.

- Is there ample staff **parking**? Is your car going to be blocked in on a regular basis? Do you have to get out of your car every morning to open and close the staff gates? This is not a deal-breaker as I have had to do this in a couple of schools, but it's not fun when it's winter, dark and you're fiddling with the combination code on a padlock with cold, numb hands!

- Are the **staff toilets** equipped with the basics? Although unusual, I worked in a school where staff felt obliged to provide soap themselves, because this building was in a block that seemed to be ignored due to its distance from the main building. Even if you don't need the toilet during your visit, make certain that you check the facilities out. Of course, if you've already decided within seconds of your visit that the school does not appeal to you, you needn't bother.

- Is there a designated **purpose-built medical room**? Are there **defibrillators** present?

- Whilst you are visiting, look at the **displays** and the **quality of pupils' handwriting and content?** If the population of the school is diverse, is diversity celebrated? Is there awareness of different languages spoken within the school? Is there evidence of cultural displays, such as themed religious and festival displays? Are there any glaring punctuation and grammatical errors on display? This will indicate staff's attention to detail and English standards. I don't wish to come across as pernickety but when visiting a school, I believe that it is important to sweat the small stuff. Displays are highly visible; therefore, a lack of proofreading in this area does not give a good impression of the school's quality of education.

- Do the **displays** give Leonardo Da Vinci or Michelangelo a run for their money? If the displays are too razzle-dazzle, it could mean that there isn't a balance of consideration from SLT for other teacher tasks. Touring the school in its entirety will give you a clearer picture in this respect.

- Is it a school heavily dependent on **ready-made** resources? What are their reasons for doing so? There are some schools that buy in schemes for maths and foundation subjects to ease the teaching load, and many of these work well for the pupils concerned; however, teachers should ensure that they adapt planning to meet the needs of their pupils and not just blindly follow a scheme wholesale.

- If possible, try to visit the school during school hours, as you will not obtain a good picture of the school without the children in it. Observe **lesson starts** and **ends** and see how the children interact with their peers at **break** and **lunchtimes.** Do the children look happy? Are they playing nicely together or are there tears and rough play? Are the staff on duty engaging with the children or are they huddled together amongst themselves, as if trying to avoid engaging with the children? During the visit, observe what the **teaching and learning** look like in the school? What is the learning intention or objective? Bear in mind that if you're visiting towards the end of a term, then you may find that the lessons are less structured; however, during a normal timetable, lessons should be **purposeful** and **knowledge-rich**. During lessons, do the students look happy, attentive and engaged? Is there relaxed alertness? Are the students asking probing questions? Is there high-quality pupil talk? Are they speaking clearly and in full sentences? Is there evidence of consolidation? Are the teachers addressing misconceptions? Has the teacher included different learning styles within the lesson? Do the adults in the classrooms look as if they are enjoying their time with the children? Do they show a true joy for teaching or are they clock-watching? In short, **are staff and students working together**?

- Be a bit like a spy! If you have gone to visit a school in the morning and you liked it, it may be worthwhile returning to the school at **home time**, parking up somewhere nearby to see how the children and parents behave beyond the school gates.

- Be aware of a school that on the day of the school tour **shields you** from the **realities** of the school by confining you to the staffroom during lesson transitions.

- Are staff expected to provide prescriptive **written lesson plans**? Even though Ofsted do not require written lesson plans, there are still some schools that demand written lesson plans on a prescriptive template, which is a pain. When I first started my teaching career, it was comforting and useful to have a lesson outline but, with experience, I found that I no longer required a written lesson plan. Planning is part and parcel of the job, and I do plan but not in a prescriptive, tick-box way. I plan a well-sequenced unit overview in a simple form and ensure that my teaching slides reflect my planning; in short, my slides double up as lesson plans. Nowadays, I only provide a lesson outline or plan for a cover teacher/supply teacher in the event of a planned absence, as my slides are sufficiently detailed and provide step-by-step guidance for both pupils and teachers.

- If you end up in the staffroom, **talk with the teachers** during your visit but don't grill them, and ensure that you read the room! Be personable and gently ask them about how they work if the opportunity presents itself; for example: How do year teams work together? Is there **joint PPA** for year teams? What resources are used? When the staff interact with you, do they seem genuinely passionate about teaching? Not all teachers are dedicated teachers wishing to be the best version of themselves, doing the best for their students. There are some teachers out there who are work-shy or have been so traumatised by the profession that they are now jaded and cynical and do as little as possible in order to survive. During a tour of the school, you probably won't have the opportunity for a lengthy discussion; however, if you are called for interview and find yourself at a loose end, delicately engage with staff and gauge their thoughts about their workplace. If staff are not particularly welcoming, perhaps the school is not for you.

Wellbeing is Not Cake and One-off Events!

- Be wary of force-fed fun schools and incidental **wellbeing** add-ons. Avoid schools where wellbeing is tantamount to sweet treats, yoga, painting, Indian head massage and dressing up, as these do very little for people's wellbeing on a long-term basis. I am partial to cake but it's hardly healthy and does not help me in any way with my workload. You need to pinpoint how the school is addressing the **wellbeing** of its staff. Is staff wellbeing even a priority in the advert? Is there ample opportunity for staff to connect socially in a relaxed manner? You want to work in a school where there is a consistent, authentic culture of wellbeing, not inconsistent, ad hoc, tick-box tokenistic approaches to wellbeing. Are high levels of care and compassion extended to the adults as well as the children? More autonomy, specifically in terms of self-governing one's own time, is the gift that all staff in a school warmly receive. When leaders provide extra PPA or cancel a meeting because there's been a lot going on in school, teachers are always relieved and grateful. In recent years, some schools have introduced report writing days, and Occasional Days, which I have appreciated. Slowly, some schools are turning to the idea of allowing teachers to have PPA off-site, which might be ideal for some teachers. Personally, I prefer to do my planning at home, as I have sometimes found PPA at school distracting due to interruptions such as telephone calls and being called out for behavioural reasons.

- Does the school make certain that there is a cut off point for **email delivery**? I don't look at emails sent after 17:00 and certainly not at the weekend, but if a school ensures that emails are only permitted to be sent from Monday to Friday between 07:00 and 17:00, it sends a clear message to everyone that they deserve to switch off from work-related tasks.

- Do staff receive adequate **PPA** time? Are there comprehensive schemes of work to support planning and teaching? Are music, PE, PSHE, RE, computing and MFL taught by subject specialists? This is worth considering because workload is further reduced when a school has **specialist staff** to teach certain foundation subjects. Not having to teach PE certainly does wonders for my mental wellbeing!

- Do staff have to be armed with **three different pens** and an **assortment of highlighters,** or is the **marking** a simpler, pared down version with one pen alongside marking **symbols/codes**?

- Check the school timetable to determine the length of lessons and **lunch**. Most schools have their timetables on their websites. During a day of supply, I worked in a secondary school where the lunch was only 45 minutes long! I would not wish to permanently work in a school with such a short lunchtime.

- Does SLT recognise **pinch points** within the academic year, or do they have several off-timetable events within any given week, which invariably means staff are just expected to juggle and maintain the ridiculous work treadmill? A good school will carefully map out the academic year and will always consider school-related events through the lens of workload; otherwise, staff will suffer burnout and go off sick. At the very least, schools should ensure that there are no meetings during the week Parents' Evenings are held.

- You have to learn the art of **reading between the lines** when reading job advertisements. Beware of schools that seek someone who 'goes the extra mile', because most teachers already go the extra mile; therefore, this likely means that they'll want every drop of blood out of you, such as driving the school van, doing after-school clubs, compelling you to attend events that, ordinarily, would be attended by volunteers or organised by PTAs. Be wary of the phrase 'We're like a family' in school adverts, as this often means that you will be expected to have an inexhaustible pool of goodwill and to participate in or organise lots of extra-curricular activities. In schools, it is important to remain a 'flexible friend' and volunteer, but this should not become a regular occurrence which burdens staff. You are not conjoined to the school and deserve to have a life that is separate from school. Whilst there will be occasions when you will have to work weekends, such as writing school reports or curriculum design, your weekends should not be continually compromised, as you need time to rest and refuel, and no job should be at the expense of your health.

Believe me, you do not want to become like a humourless shadow of your former self because you're overworked and deeply unhappy.

- A school which constantly uses the refrain **'It's for the children'** so that you sacrifice yourself and put yourself last is not a good place in which to work, and one could argue that this is emotional blackmail: manipulating staff to work beyond what is deemed reasonable. I have even heard of teachers who mark their books whilst away on holiday. I plan units of lessons during the holidays as I find it more relaxing than planning reactively every day after school, but I **never** mark books during my holiday, whether I am away or not. Don't allow this sort of toxic indoctrination to seep in as it could lead to burnout. In the eyes of the school, you are not indispensable, and you can be easily replaced, with the memory of your name and contributions soon forgotten. **You are not wedded to your job,** and you will be no good to anyone, least of all yourself, if you don't look after yourself. One of my husband's favourite maxims is "Nothing works, unless you do".

Behaviour

This is an extremely important feature of a school life and some of the approaches to whole-school behaviour management I have seen in my lifetime have not been entirely sensible to me. Misbehaviour is often the red line for teachers and one of the common reasons for educators leaving the profession. Without effective behaviour systems, a school is pretty much doomed, and you become de-skilled as a teacher because all you end up doing is firefighting and literally raising your blood pressure. To hone your craft, you need to have the freedom to teach the masses and not have your time monopolised by students who are resistant to reasonable behavioural expectations. You do not want to work in a school where it is acceptable for students to ignore you, defy you and bully you, and each day becomes an inevitable, toxic

Groundhog Day. Such vampire schools only drain the lifeblood of both staff and students, which then leads to a general air of malaise. During my NQT (Newly Qualified Teacher as it was then known) year, I worked in what was generally considered a 'tough' school, but it was manageable because there was always a member of SLT on call with two-way radios to extract students who would or could not behave during lessons. This provided respite for both teachers and the students who wanted to learn. Also, you were not expected to produce a trail of paperwork afterwards, just a code and short explanation of what happened on the computerised behaviour system. It was simple and not onerous. Any system that expects you to do paperwork in triplicate will grind you down.

I reiterate: You do not want to work in a school where abuse of staff from students and parents is the norm. Having your lessons derailed or hijacked by uncooperative, boisterous students causes harm to the students who want to learn and is a sure and steady path to becoming thoroughly de-skilled as a teacher. There are sadly numerous schools of this type in existence.

Behaviour Policies

Unfortunately, behavioural expectations vary widely across schools. Some policies read well but schools do not always carry out what they say on the tin when it comes to behaviour, whereas others can be a bit namby-pamby and convoluted. Nowadays, many schools incorporate values and mottoes with the intention to inform positive conduct and learning behaviours; however, these values are not always translated around the school. Usually, this is because these mottoes and values can be a bit woolly and vague, and are not modelled in a way that pupils can visibly see on a daily basis. In my husband's primary school, they had two mottoes: "Only the best is good enough," and "If at first you don't succeed, try and try again." He has never forgotten them!

One of the things to consider when reading the **behaviour policy** on the school's website is whether it has been written in Plain English or child-friendly terms. During your visit, see if this behaviour policy is fully embedded, such as teachers using keywords from the policy. Is there a **shared language (a script)** amongst staff with which students are familiar?

Some schools talk about their school being a **'nurturing'** environment and I agree with nurturing young people, as I am dedicated to helping pupils develop their sense of civic duty, supporting them and guiding them, helping them to flourish, learn and grow; however, unfortunately, the word 'nurturing' in some schools often translates as 'indulging' children. Pandering to children sets the bar extremely low in terms of behavioural expectations and socially stunts them, most likely rendering them unemployable in the future. I am not saying for a minute that pastoral care or specific behavioural needs should be sidelined; however, I would argue that a school is not meeting its pastoral duty if persistently misbehaving students are unable to communicate effectively, read fluently, write well, socialise with others or do basic maths when they leave school. In other words, the school is not providing an environment that allows such students to thrive socially and academically and is doing a disservice to such pupils.

A simple set of behaviour steps (maximum of five steps, as any more can be difficult for pupils and staff to remember) written in child-friendly terms with **precise** language works best. Working in an environment where SLT support their teachers to teach by creating the conditions for successful learning and having clear systems, that all parties understand and follow, helps to create a calm, happy environment which is conducive to learning. In short, you want to work in a school where pupils and staff are working from the same hymn sheet and the behaviour system is easy-to-understand and follow.

Type of School and Training Opportunities

What **kind of school** is it? Is it an independent school, single academy or MAT, free school, religious school or local authority-managed (L.A.) school? Some MATs provide a high level of support to senior leaders, particularly within domains such as recruitment, training and finances, and provide a range of free course packages for MAT staff. However, do look at reviews about the trust concerned, as not all trusts and free schools are high-performing organisations. If you are considering working in a trust, free school or private school, it is worth checking the financial health of the school by checking its details on **Companies House**. Job security is important, especially in these precarious times.

I have worked in a few academies, and in two of the three where I taught, there was no significant difference in employment conditions, as pay and pensions remained the same. Nevertheless, do bear in mind that some MATs and free schools can be more **corporate** in their approach as they will not always following the teaching unions' stance on work conditions and pay, and will trim the fat wherever possible. Also, in academies and free schools, there can be many proverbial 'cooks' in senior management – CEO, executive headteacher/principal, directors of learning, head of school, phase leads, etc. This is not necessarily negative; however, when the aforementioned are working in isolation rather than collaboratively and are sending you emails or requests that are duplications of what you have received from others within the SLT chain, then having to respond to communications left, right and centre from several members of leadership only adds to workload and wastes significant time.

Teaching should be an evolutionary profession and, therefore, you want to work in a school that is forward-thinking and innovative, always seeking to improve its teaching practice for the betterment of its students. Is the school cultivating its staff through purposeful training as well as **vertical** and **lateral** progression opportunities? Is training tailored to meet the needs of the staff or is it training that has been foisted upon all staff? Top-down training does not always work; opt-in training is much more effective. Schools cannot please everyone; therefore, I would advise you to keep abreast of your own CPD including keeping a copy of your training records off-site.

How many **meetings** are held per week? If you want to consider your life outside of school, it is a question that needs to be asked. You don't want to feel completely wrung out every day of the working week. I worked in a school which had three weekly meetings: one was a weekly **teacher meeting** (1hr 30mins) which was developmental; a **year group meeting** (1hr); and a **teacher briefing** for the week ahead (10-15mins) during Friday lunchtime. Thankfully, I was not a member of SLT at this school as I dread to think what the total number of meetings for members of SLT was. Furthermore, are staff expected to travel to other schools for meetings/coaching/training? Having a car and clean driving licence is important for teachers, because if you work within a multi-academy trust, you may be required to travel to other schools within the trust, which may not always be easily accessible by public transport.

Go with Your Gut!

If something does not feel right, don't proceed with the application even if you can't exactly explain why. Likewise, if you decide to apply and land a job that you soon discover is a nightmare, get out as soon as possible! **Life is too short** to spend in an environment that is harmful and detrimental to your health. Your health is your wealth. It is vital that you have some money saved for a rainy day, should you leave a role without another job lined up. If you do end up job-hopping because you refuse to settle and are striving to find a good match for you, make certain that you retain all the **positive references** you collect along the way. Unfortunately, certain headteachers do abuse their power, lack integrity, and behave unprofessionally when staff leave their school, producing references which are a work of fiction in an attempt to sabotage future careers. If you have a bank of great references and written lesson feedback forms, you can offset any inaccurate or false references. If you do decide to apply, you could attach copies of your positive references to the application or use extracts from your references in the body of your application to support your teaching statement. For interviews, I carry a **teaching portfolio** which contains references, a copy of my CV, pupils' work, planning extracts, letters and cards from pupils.

Very early on in my teaching career, one of the schools where I worked closed, primarily due to dwindling pupil numbers. I remember the first staff meeting I attended as a new member of staff, raring to go, and the headteacher opened with: "The school is in crisis." He did not sugar-coat it, and my jaw almost dropped. This happened a long time ago, before the internet was the powerful, dominating force that it is today but, from that day forth, I endeavoured to critique schools through questioning and research to minimise the chances of ending up in a nightmarish school. Over the years, this has become easier because of the World Wide Web and school visits.

Moreover, **thoroughly check what the school's curriculum looks like beforehand** because I made the mistake of working in a school that alternated its cross-curricular curriculum, which meant that no two years were the same; for example, whilst there, I taught Year 5 consecutively for two years, and then Year 4 consecutively for two years, but each year was totally different because of the school's bi-annual topic-based curriculum. Although I liked the topic-based approach, it was extremely time-consuming and mentally taxing, as all subjects had to be taught through a topic; for example, if the topic was 'The Maya', *every* subject had to be Mayan in theme not just history; therefore mathematical word problems had to be Mayan in theme, music had to be Mayan in theme, even science lessons had to link to the Maya. The work did not stop there, though, as classroom displays also had to be changed each term in accordance with the change of topics, which were changed on a termly basis; for example, in one year, I taught the following three topics: World War Two, Pompeii, and Ancient Egypt across all subjects. Furthermore, this school did not permit joint planning because they did not want 'cookie-cutter' lessons. This meant that teachers worked in isolation and good practice was not properly shared. The workload was off the charts! Once you make the mistake of working in an organisation of this nature, you won't ever want to repeat it.

A word of advice: If you end up working in a school that you enjoy, half enjoy or at least find tolerable, there are some **benefits to staying put**, as you will become **more established** with each passing year and **build stronger relationships** with staff, parents and children. From a behaviour standpoint, pupils are more likely to behave for you when they see you as **part of the furniture**. If you remain in the same year group for a few years, then this can ease your workload immensely, as the repetition of the curriculum allows you to fine-tune your lesson delivery and refine your planning. This process allows you to evaluate the previous year's planning and decide what worked well and what didn't work so well. In other words, you won't have to start over again in a new workplace with new planning, systems and faces, which will free up your time.

Another piece of advice that I would like to share here is make certain that you join a **Teaching Union; this is extremely important!** So far, I have only had to seek advice from my union on one occasion early in my teaching career and the expertise I received was exceptional.

Sadly, teaching is not always a kind profession, but I hope that you find a school that makes you feel valued and included, where staff work together in concord and harmony, as there are still schools which embody these qualities. Bear in mind that no school is perfect and that you sometimes must change your **mindset** or **adjust your expectations**; for example, you may not wish to travel long distances but if the school down the road is awful whereas the school 40 minutes away is wonderful, you might want to rethink your expectations regarding travel. Above all else, remember to **value yourself,** and do not become institutionalised or indoctrinated by toxic schools.

Hopefully, the contents of this chapter will allow your thoughts to percolate before applying to a school. I think that every teacher desires and deserves to work in a school which will foster good relationships within the school community, and give you considerable time and space to think and plan memorable, meaningful lessons that meet the needs of your students. Working in a school that does not align with your values is a miserable experience. Find a school where you feel a sense of belonging. If you are currently seeking a role, I wish you well in your job search and hope that you find a role that fits you like a glove!

In a nutshell:

1. Be **inquisitive**! There is a great deal to think about when considering vacancies and you need to ensure that you read between the lines when looking at job adverts.

2. **Avoid rushing and be patient!** Decide what your deal-breakers are. You need to build sufficient knowledge of the school on which to base a **decision**. Don't just barrel into the first job you see, as alignment is vital. Do your due diligence and be forensic in your approach to evaluating a school. Remember to harness the power of the internet!

3. Undertake a pre-application visit, if you wish, or watch school videos to find out as much as you can about the school. **Your instincts are valid.** Do **consider** your **internal vibe** as you navigate the school during your pre-application visit and listen to your instincts.

Searching for Teaching Jobs and Spotting Red Flags

Notes

Chapter 3
Top Ten Supply Teaching Hacks

Still looking for a teaching role? If you have not yet been able to secure a permanent teaching role or you want the opportunity to experience a range of schools, you may decide to do some supply work. One of the benefits of working as a supply teacher is that it provides insight into a wide range of schools, and sometimes supply positions can become permanent. If you work in a school and find that you like it, and a vacancy becomes available, it's a win-win for you and the school.

Supply is not always well paid as many tend to offer a lower-end fixed rate of pay, irrespective of experience; however, working with a few reputable agencies grants you wider access to a selection of schools and is a great way of seeing how other schools operate. Alternatively, you may be able to work directly with a school as a supply teacher and be paid according to MPS/UPS; some local councils have talent pools for such roles. I learned so much from working as a supply teacher about curriculum design, behaviour systems, culture and ethos. Depending on the school in which you're based, teaching can be quite an insular profession, but supply teaching allows you to see a myriad of schools and I have certainly absorbed great ideas from the schools that I visited as a supply teacher.

Here are some of my top hacks for being a successful supply teacher, or **'visiting teacher'**, which is the term I prefer due to the unfortunate negative connotations associated with supply teaching. I even wore my own **lanyard** with the words 'Visiting Teacher' in enlarged lettering to make my position visible and clear to all.

Hack 1: Travel & School

If you are not sure about the reputation of the school or distance from your home to the school, do a *Google* search and use *Google Maps,* using the arrive time feature in **Google Maps** to give you an idea of expected rush hour travel time. Never solely rely on the supply agency's estimation of travel time as they will often be generous to lure you in to fulfil their client's requirements.

Ensure that you make a mental or physical note of the senior leadership team and check out the behavioural policy, so that you know what to do in the event of severe misbehaviour. If the school's policy behaviour is not clear, use your common sense, such as change the seating, etc., and seek assistance from the SLT, if necessary.

Hack 2: Arrival & Resources

Although agencies will often tell you to arrive by 08:15, I would arrive earlier (around 08:00) to get the lay of the land, as you never know what you'll be confronted with. I would not arrive before 08:00 as reception staff generally do not man front of house until 08:00. Organised schools usually have a one-page A4 summary, leaflet or folder for supply teachers that contains key information, such as medical notes and specific learning needs. For supply jobs, I always carried my **A5 page-a-day diary** and **writing pen** in my handbag for ease of access, just in case I had to sign in manually or take notes quickly.

Arriving early gives you sufficient time to obtain computer access details, medical lists, locate the toilets, speak to staff, source a laptop, paper and even quickly plan a morning maths challenge and lessons for the day, if resources have not been left. I've worked in schools where no slides were provided, no planning set, or the planning left had so little educational substance that I didn't want a part of it. I have even had to search high and low for a laptop like a blue-arsed fly, as not all schools have in-situ computers in classrooms.

Check to see whether the teacher has left seating plans but do not worry if seating plans have not been left, particularly in the primary sector, as pupils will usually follow the seating plan without reminders. If you are not happy with some of the seating, you are perfectly within your rights to change the seating arrangement to suit your expectations.

I recall one occasion when three differentiated worksheets had been copied but they had not been separated according to the level of challenge. I only realised this when it came to the distribution of the worksheets. Also, the colouring pencils required for the task were nowhere to be seen which meant I had to ask the neighbouring class for theirs. This lack of organisation wasted valuable learning time and did not facilitate good behaviour, as pupils became bored whilst I was sorting out the worksheets. So, my advice would be to double-check that the resources have been well organised, and all the equipment needed for the tasks is readily available before the class arrives, wherever possible.

During my teaching training, trainees were taught that cover lessons had to be planned well and that when planning cover lessons, it was essential they were lessons **anyone** could deliver. Ten plus years ago, this was the case as solid black and white consolidation lessons (which required little or no preparation for supply staff) were generally provided but this is rarely the case nowadays. In this climate, you will have to be super flexible, frequently think on your feet and be prepared to adapt ill-prepared lessons for lessons to be purposeful. It is particularly disappointing when a ready-made worksheet is milked for all its worth because whoever set cover could or would not prepare additional work. Such poor planning does adversely impact on behaviour as pupils' concentration will wane if faced with two hours of doing the same task. In these circumstances, as a supply teacher I would make up extension tasks linked to the topic, search for short videos to reinforce a learning point and use my own resources from my USB stick, if necessary.

However, there may be occasions when the absent teacher is short on time for the completion of a unit and decide that they want the supply teacher to pick up from they left off; for example, a writing unit that they're in the middle of that needs to be continued in their absence. For the supply lesson to go smoothly, the absent teacher (or his/her colleagues) will need to provide detailed instructions as to what happened previously to set up the supply teacher and pupils for success. One way of doing this would be to provide the **previous slides** and a sample of **high-quality pupils' work highlighting skills** learned in the most recent lessons, with a **model** for the supply lesson so that both the supply teacher and pupils know exactly which skills they are practising. Unfortunately, I have worked in schools where I have been told to model on the hoof. To produce excellent learning outcomes, models should be strategically planned, not improvised.

Hack 3: Register

Upon arrival, ask if supply teachers have access to an electronic register. If yes, ask what kind of software is used; for example, *Arbor*, *SIMS*, *Google* or *Excel* sheet, as you need someone to show you if you are not familiar with the aforementioned. If the answer is no, kindly ask for a paper register there and then, as it avoids having to wait for a child to retrieve it from the office. It is fine to ask a pupil for a register in the afternoon but in the morning, there is often a great deal going on, such as lunchtime options and morning assembly.

Hack 4: Disclosure Barring Service (DBS)

Technically, the school should be with the DBS update service, and you should only have to provide your registration number; however, nearly all schools I visited requested a copy of my paper DBS certificate, so ensure that you carry your certificate in a protective wallet or case.

Hack 5: Set the Tone

Check you know how to operate the interactive board as you do not want to be faffing around, sorting out technical issues in the presence of the pupils; it does not set a good tone for the start of the day. Warmly greet the pupils as they enter and have your name clearly written on the whiteboard prior to their arrival. Once pupils have settled, make your expectations clear from the outset and formally introduce yourself.

Use alliteration and repetition when instructing pupils to ensure that what you're saying is memorable and catchy; for example, 'kind hands, kind feet'. For those of you familiar with the work of Doug Lemov's *Teach Like a Champion*, you might wish to use a variation of SLANT (**S**itting up straight, **L**istening attentively, **A**nswering questions, **N**ever interrupting, **T**racking the adult). Follow the school's behaviour policy; if this is not visible, ask for a copy upon arrival at the school.

Try to learn the pupils' names. If you find it difficult to memorise pupils' names, ask pupils to record their names on a Post-it note and to stick it on the desk in front of them. If there are no Post-it notes available, some pieces of paper cut into strips will do. If you are lucky enough to have teaching assistants, ensure that you introduce yourself to them, show gratitude and involve them in the lessons. Ask them if any of the pupils have medical needs (especially important if the school office did not provide this information previously) and what the home time rules are, as every school is different; for example, some schools allow Years 5 and 6 to walk home alone but other schools don't. Some schools issue passwords to parents as part of their safeguarding procedures. For this system, it is imperative that the adults collecting children know the password for the children to be released to them.

Hack 6: Stationery

When I did supply work, I carried my teaching materials in a plain black **backpack**. In terms of stationery, always carry a pack of **whiteboard pens of different colours**, as I entered many classrooms during supply assignments to find either nearly expired whiteboard pens or worse, a total absence of whiteboard pens. For marking, ensure that you bring green, black, blue, purple, red and pink pens for marking, as not all schools use green for teacher marking. If it is easier, you could purchase a **BIC 4 colours ballpoint pen**.

I also carried **spare pencils**, some **lined paper**, **plain paper**, and a couple of **envelopes** in case I had to leave anything of a private and confidential nature for the class teacher. For the recording of assignments, I would carry a **page-a-day A5 diary** to keep track of supply assignments, etc., and this would often double up as a general notebook.

Unfortunately, some classrooms that I entered as a supply teacher were so cluttered and messy that there was little surface area to arrange resources in a neat pile. Thankfully, most of the whiteboards in schools are magnetic; therefore, I used **magnetic buttons** to put the cover outline and a copy of each printed resource on the board. This meant that I didn't mix up the cover outline with resources and, if resources ended up buried underneath mountains of clutter, I had quick access to the agenda for the day and could photocopy spare copies, if needed. If you don't have magnetic buttons, a magnetic whiteboard eraser will suffice.

Hack 7: Textbooks

When liaising with your agency or school, specify the year groups you wish to teach and pack textbooks accordingly. For example, in primary settings, I only wanted to work with Year 3 to Year 6; therefore, I carried maths textbooks specific to those year groups. In the absence of planning, these textbooks were very useful as I could use them as a springboard for ideas and the foundation for a solid lesson. I will take you through my resource staples in Chapter 8.

You may also wish to bring a reading book of short stories so that you can read to the class at the end of the day, just in case there isn't a class reader book available.

Hack 8: Marking

It never ceased to amaze me how certain teachers did not provide answers for differentiated maths worksheets when they knew supply would be covering; therefore, I always brought a maths calculator in case I needed to work out the answers in advance, so that I could then share the answers with pupils and instruct them to self-mark.

In supply teaching, it is not uncommon to be left with a pile of marking at the end of the day, as some teachers unfairly cram as much as they can when they know supply is in to ease their workload. Some of the teachers for whom I was covering would stipulate in their covering plans that marking be done yet provide no mark schemes for closed tasks. Furthermore, to add insult to injury, when looking through books (particularly Foundation exercise books) very little marking or acknowledgement marking had been done previously by the teacher. In one school where I did supply, the teacher requested that I teach double English and maths, which certainly increased my workload for the day.

Most supply agencies only pay for 6.5 hours, which does not consider the extra hours after school devoted to marking. To reduce workload, instruct the pupils to self-assess with their editing pens; use the visualiser to share answers for maths, spellings and Guided Reading comprehension questions; try to do as much live marking as possible during lessons; and mark during part of your lunch hour (don't forget to eat, drink and care for yourself too). I suggest that you always bring your own lunch and drink. Also, ensure that you stamp children's books with a 'Supply Teacher' stamp as it is immediately visible to the pupils and shows that you have acknowledged pupils' books. Stamping is also useful for the class teacher as SLT will be able to differentiate between the class teacher's lessons and supply-led lessons.

If the work requires detailed marking, such as narrative writing, correct work and provide comments, if necessary, by using the school's choice of pen colours and following the school's marking policy. If you cannot find the school's marking policy, look at the previous work that the teacher has marked for guidance. For generic positive comments, there is a plethora of **classroom stamps** that you can buy online to reduce marking load. In the past, I have used *Classroom Capers* and *Amazon* (please see Chapter 1 for the list of stamps that I use).

Sadly, there are some supply teachers who routinely do not mark books and leave the premises as soon as the children have been dismissed, but if you do this, chances are that you will not secure repeat custom and you may not be the agency's first port of call.

Hack 9: Visualiser & USB Stick

Not all classrooms have visualisers; therefore, it is a good idea to bring a **portable visualiser** with you. I would wrap my portable visualiser in protective bubble wrap and store it in a large pencil case or bag when transporting it between schools.

You can model effectively under a visualiser, show maths answers/workings and read a story with the class under the visualiser so that pupils can follow the story as you read. Whenever I took out my visualiser in schools that did not have one, I was always greeted with happy gasps of astonishment; it's a cracking tool to have!

Have a **USB stick** containing your most successful lessons; for example, for my supply lessons, I have the following signature lessons for KS2 maths:

- Short multiplication
- Percentages
- Decimals
- Equivalent fractions
- Factors
- Area

For English:
- Diary writing
- Personification poetry
- Persuasive writing
- Character description
- Drafting and editing
- SPaG – adjectival usage
- Reading comprehension questions: *A Visit to Baba Yaga* (a Russian folk tale) – this always goes down well.

For science, I have a few lessons on classification but if there is access to tablets or laptops, I instruct the pupils to research the interesting scientists below and share videos of each scientist via *BBC Bitesize:*

- Katherine Johnson
- Mary Anning
- Isaac Newton
- Galileo Galilei

For French:
- Greetings
- Colours
- Alphabet
- Numbers

To further engage pupils, I would also use *BBC Bitesize* and refer to the *Dorling Kindersley 'DK findout!'* website https://www.dk.com/uk/category/dkfindout/ which features high-quality images across a wide range of subjects in an interactive way.

Hack 10: Handover Notes & Tidying

When I did supply, I thanked the teaching assistants, pupils, and the teacher for whom I was covering for their resources (if they left any) and cover plan. I also wrote some brief comments about my day with the class concerned, such as work covered, highlights and behaviour, for the purposes of continuity. I created an easy-to-use **handover template** that I will share with you in Chapter 5.

Maintain **classroom tidiness** throughout the day by instructing pupils to tidy up after themselves and **never ever leave the classroom in an untidy state at the end of the day**. I keep in mind the teacher for whom I am covering, especially if they have been off due to illness; imagine how it would feel to return to a classroom in a messy state. This happened to me once as I returned to my classroom to find broken blinds, books not returned to their rightful place, broken pencils and pens strewn across the floor at the back, torn posters, etc. In short, it was not left as it was first found. If you leave a classroom in a bad state, it is likely that the teacher for whom you were covering will complain and you will not be asked back.

Top Tip: Whenever you leave cover work for supply staff, try to be as helpful as possible and ensure lessons are easy to follow.

In a nutshell:

1. Be **open** to supply teaching if you have not yet managed to secure a permanent teaching position.

2. Be **clear** about the year groups you wish to teach, and **mark** pupils' work where applicable.

3. Be **prepared**! Ensure that you have back-up lesson plans in case no planning has been left.

Top Ten Supply Teaching Hacks

Notes

Chapter 4
Drop Dazzling Displays!

"Perfection is achieved, not when there is nothing more to add, but when there is nothing left to take away." - Antoine de Saint-Exupery French writer (1900–1944)

When I think about a classroom, I sometimes cast my mind back to my childhood when I used to watch *The Waltons*, and the teacher taught from the front to a mixed-age class in a small wooden cabin with a greenish blackboard and chalk. Nothing adorned the walls or desks. This classroom scene is not dissimilar to certain classrooms in poorer parts of the world. In many of these spartan classrooms, learning is evident, and knowledge is revered; so why in the UK, are so many classrooms overly complicated and cluttered when it is clear that children can learn successfully in the most barren of environments? Children don't need to feast on pretty visuals, as my time in the classroom shows that they are perfectly happy with a kind, caring, patient teacher who imparts knowledge. Central to this chapter is the fact that over-the-top displays do not underpin good teaching or relationships in the classroom. You want your classroom to be an attractive and inviting place to be, but your classroom needn't be an art installation or explosion in a paint factory. Children should feast on knowledge, not pretty pictures. My past and present students are living proof that you do **not** need pretentious displays for successful learning outcomes in the classroom. I am guilty of having erected stunning displays that the children were wowed by when initially unveiled; however, by the end of the day (once the novelty faded away) they barely glanced at them. Love them or loathe them, whatever your stance on displays, they are generally regarded as a staple of classrooms, particularly in primary schools. What we need to be mindful of is that these display boards should be for the children's benefit, not vanity projects. Your display **should never be cluttered,** as visual clutter is not helpful to your children, particularly those who are neurodivergent.

Here are some photographs of past vanity projects:

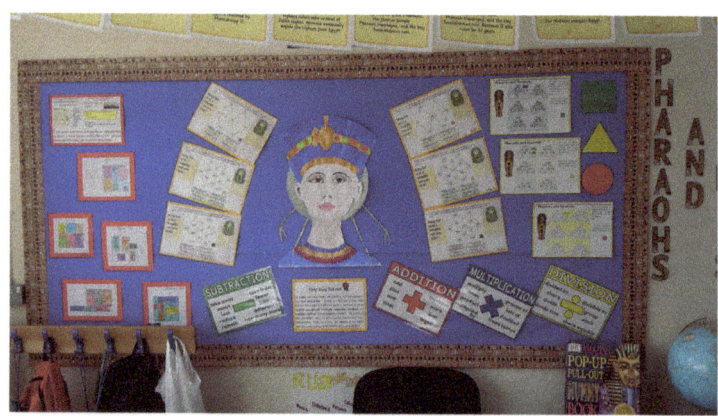

Picture 16: Vanity Projects – Avoid these types of displays!

I was lucky at the school where these photos were taken as I could print off my ideas and images taken from the internet and then relay what I wanted to my talented TA, and it would magically happen. The above shows a sample of the children's work across a range of abilities, but there is no exemplification to show the class why the work has been successful. The Nefertiti image, which dominates the display, has little impact on learning. The photos shown here, featuring bold artwork with 3D elements and eye-catching slogans, are better placed in the corridor for the school community and visitors to view examples of pupils' work, rather than in the classroom. In the classroom, you must be relentless and consistent in what truly matters in terms of learning in the classroom. Do not be drawn into **superficial** display boards or worse, engage in unhealthy, unspoken 'Who has the best display?' competitions with colleagues. Your classroom does not need to be an art exhibition.

Thankfully, there's been a noticeable shift away from the evangelism of fixed displays, as many schools have now adopted 'Working Walls' that are current and reflect the learning in the classroom rather than presenting static, magnificent works of art. Every classroom display should serve as a learning tool that children routinely use to help them in their learning. If your displays are not offering concrete support for learning, then they have no purpose, and your time could have been better spent elsewhere.

In this chapter, I seek to demystify displays and share with you what I do in my Key Stage 2 classroom to boost learning, reduce workload and save time. It's no frills but it yields fantastic results, and you can customise what I've provided to suit you and your pupils. I use the same display **templates** every year and tweak here and there; in short, I am a creature of habit and use **formulae**, and I want to share this with you because if this display blueprint works for me, then I think it will work for you, too. When it comes to displays, I ensure that my classroom is welcoming and aesthetically pleasing but I trim the fat; otherwise, displays can soon devour your time. Using my own branded templates is something I use in many facets of my teaching; namely, my PowerPoint teaching slides, lesson overviews, homework and worksheets which I discuss later in the next chapter. I find that the automation of using the same font, colour-scheme, line thickness, graphics and *Bitmojis*, makes life so much easier and it provides routine for both my pupils and me.

Look Around Your Classroom

Firstly, before you even consider covering your display boards in backing paper, survey your classroom and find the vantage points and the blind spots, as there is no point displaying materials in areas of the room that can't be seen clearly by all pupils.

Colour of Backing Paper

To create a clean, visually uncluttered yet welcoming, warm, dyslexic-friendly working environment, I stick to **one colour** for the backing of my display boards. I like the uniformity of yellow or cream as my go-to colour with simple black lettering, because yellow or cream combined with black or blue lettering is dyslexic-friendly. I like to keep things simple and will affix a black border to all display boards, but this is dependent on the availability of resources at your school. I am a firm believer that whatever works for dyslexic students will work for all; minimalism is key! I adopt the same method in my PowerPoints, which I will discuss in due course.

Top Tip: If the original backing paper has been left up, you can use this to measure the length of new backing paper needed. Don't worry too much about the state of the edges when cutting, as you can cover a multitude of raggedy sins with the border.

Lettering

Alliterative titles for display boards are memorable and can be used as a starting point when discussing alliteration as a literary device in writing. I like to think that everything displayed in my classroom has a learning purpose. In terms of dyslexic-friendly fonts, I like Century Gothic and TW Century MT but there are many others you can choose from. Here are some common dyslexic-friendly fonts, because they are sans serif.

- Comic Sans
- Gill Sans MT
- **Berlin Sans FB**
- Cavolini
- Century Gothic
- TW Cen MT
- TW Cent MT Condensed
- Segoe Print
- Bradley Hand IT

When I first started primary teaching, I used to link the fonts with the topic; for example, if the topic was 'Vikings', I would spend considerable time trying to find a runic-looking font, but I abandoned this approach a long time ago as it is not purposeful and wastes time.

I tend to use my working walls for maths, English, science and MFL. In a previous classroom, I had fewer display boards; therefore, I focused on maths and English. Here are the common titles that I use for my display boards in Century Gothic, black, font size 450, landscape orientation so that I can fit more letters onto one page of A4 paper. To reduce plastic usage and time, I do not laminate lettering.

- Marvellous Maths
- Exciting English or Wonderful Writing
- Sensational Science

For the 'Sensational Science' board, I affix subject-specific vocabulary and images related to the topic under discussion.

Before the end of the academic year, if I have time, I print these titles off and cut out at home. In the past, I have even roped members of my family into helping me cut out individual letters. Another hack if you don't have time to individually cut around letters, is to place the lettering together and then cut around it as a group of letters.

Top Tip 1: On the back of each cut-out letter, lightly number the back of each letter in pencil, as this will support with the organisation of the lettering. Next, carefully paper clip and put in envelopes to avoid inadvertent creasing.

Top Tip 2: Before you begin to affix letters, place blobs of Blu Tack on the back of letters in one batch, so you don't have to keep stopping to apply Blu Tack.

Top Tip 3: If you stay in the same school, towards the end of the academic year, start preparing display materials for the subsequent year so that you don't have to go into school during the summer holiday.

One important thing to remember when preparing your display boards is not to get bogged down in fancy fonts, and make sure that certain words are spelt correctly. It is painful to see words such as 'retrieval' spelt as 'retrival' and 'separate' and 'definite' spelt as 'seperate' and 'definate', misspelt by teachers. Use a dyslexic-friendly font of your choice and **stick with it**. Century Gothic is my font of choice because it is easy-on-the-eye, dyslexic-friendly and looks clean and crisp. Being consistent with mainly one font style means I am not wasting time thinking about fancy fonts and everything around the classroom looks more uniform instead of haphazard.

Overleaf is an example of a working wall at the start of an academic year. You can see that the boards feature the yellow background I mentioned previously, with clear visuals and the same sans serif font used throughout in order to support SEND and pupils with dyslexia. Children today are generally over-stimulated by what they watch on their screens; therefore, a minimalist board is more restful on the mind and eyes. Over the years, I have reduced visual clutter in my classroom because it was often nothing more than busy wallpaper.

Picture 17: Sensational Science

Although creating beautiful displays is not a priority for me, I don't want a dog's dinner of a classroom and do have high expectations when it comes to presentation, which means backing needs to be neatly affixed to boards; work is mounted straight, not crooked. Again, this stems from my philosophy of modelling high expectations. Be selective about what you put up on your boards, too, and remember to clear old materials. You don't want a working wall to become cluttered with current learning buried under swathes of previous pieces of flipchart paper, as this defeats the purpose of what you are doing. Now that we have covered the basics, I would like to give you a flavour of what my display content is, to help you with your own set up.

Classroom Display Materials

I tend to devise my own display materials as I find it easier to tailor them to my lesson planning content, but if you do decide to use pre-made materials, ensure that they are specific to the needs of your class; proofread them thoroughly and make certain that they are dyslexic-friendly and easy to see and read from a distance.

Your school will probably insist that certain items are displayed in your classroom, such as an alphabet banner, policy posters and number line. So, what else is useful to have on classroom display boards? Below is a **step-by-step guide** to the display and presentation content that I use in the KS2 classroom that will allow you to escape from the stress of thinking about what you need to put on display in your classroom. Once you have made them, you can recycle them each year with the odd tweak.

I have split these resources into three areas:

1. English Working Wall
2. Maths Working Wall
3. Science Working Wall

Content	Text for Display	Visuals (if applicable) and comments
1. ENGLISH		
Banned words (on English board) These are the words that I want my pupils to avoid in their written work because they are not high-level. This has been a game changer in terms of supporting my pupils in both their spoken and written English because from the beginning, my pupils are taught that they need to use high-quality language in their speaking and writing, such as precise vocabulary choices,	nice big little small scary blue green red yellow cold hot happy sad walked looked shouted get got getting so see	I do not laminate these banned words. Instead, I stick the words on black backing paper to make them pop out and then I place them around a bin visual. I also add a star writer image (that I found online), a Clipart pen image and some book images to highlight the fact that it is an English board. On this working wall, I place keywords from shared writing, models and enlarged photocopies of pupils' work. A classroom

figurative language, personification, similes, etc. You need to start as you mean to go on and this is a **simple** resource which instantly tells the class the banal words to avoid. If you have time, you could colour-code the words according to word class; for example: blue for nouns pink for adjectives purple for adverbs green for verbs	saw went stuff also like (not the verb) and (repeatedly) said the (avoid using at the start of narratives)	should be language-rich and as supportive as possible. It is important for children's effective vocabulary choices work to be celebrated, and for pupils to see marked examples for them to know what made the writing successful. This is shorthand **exemplification that shows the children that you prize their contributions.** You can also scan or photograph pupils' work and insert into your PowerPoints to build a vault of pupils' work for the future. I use an app called '**PDF Extra**' (it's free if you can put up with the adverts) on my mobile phone, that allows me to scan hard copies into PDF files, but you could photograph, if you prefer.

		If your school follows Jane Considine's *The Write Stuff*, you could employ her system of 'sentence stacking' which involves selecting successful sentences from each pupil across a sequence of lessons and displaying them in the classroom, making certain that the version of the sentence you display has been edited and polished. Again, if this is the methodology your school follows, I would write this on flipchart paper for speed or use the large pre-cut strips of paper that some schools provide for this purpose.
Punctuation Personalities	Free online ready-made resource	I found the resource: 'Punctuation Personalities' on www.instantdisplay.co.uk. I laminated them and then placed them on the English board. I printed off the most relevant punctuation

		for my class rather than printing all images. The children find them useful and, if you are teaching a particular SPaG point, you can remove the laminate(s) in question and Blu-tack to the front during the teacher-input stage of your lesson.
Blank laminates	Blank	You could use off-cuts from your prior lamination work or individually cut out some strips of white/cream paper in landscape for lamination. You can then write keywords for subject-specific language. You can re-use time and time again.
Proofreading symbols (please see Chapter 6 for information on the symbols used).	At the start of every year, I teach pupils basic proofreading skills through a short PowerPoint. The symbols	I copy the slide from my PowerPoint and enlarge it to A3 to make a poster.

	work well alongside my school's marking policy; therefore, it makes marking more manageable and purposeful.	
Pupil Voice speech bubble	This is a laminated resource that I can re-use for years, if not sun-bleached. I place it next to my English board. During certain units of work, I seek feedback from my pupils which they write on Post-it notes. Once they have finished writing their feedback on their Post-it notes, they place it under the speech bubble.	Again, I created this in PowerPoint using the 'Shapes' feature. *Picture 18: Pupil Voice*

	This is often thoughtful, considered feedback which informs my planning.	
Handwriting banner	The lower-case alphabet banner I use is from *Nelson Handwriting* software. The handwriting style you use will depend on your whole school's handwriting policy as some schools follow other schemes, such as *Letter-join*. I did not laminate it. I just stuck the sheets together to create a banner.	My banner is nothing fancy, but it does the job as the children do refer to it, if needed, to remind them of formation and joins. I highlight the letters in bright blue that do not join, and this is placed above my English Working Wall.

Imagination Station This is the title for my reading corner which I Blu-tacked to the wall.	Imagination Station	I found some black and white clipart photos of butterflies that I liked. Then I cut them out and made them 3D. For reasons of copyright, I cannot share a detailed image here, but this is what the finished wall looked like.  *Picture 19: Reading Corner*
2. MATHS		
Maths Operations This resource presents the four operations with corresponding specific vocabulary relevant to each operation. This resource is bold and easy to read.	Details of the ready-made resource: Addition has a red frame Subtraction – green frame Multiplication – blue frame	Visit www.instant. display This supports pupils' understanding of word problems. I also stick some maths-related images, such as a ruler, protractor, calculator, etc. Although I like minimalism, I don't want my classroom to be too clinical for my pupils; therefore, a

	Division – yellow frame	few images related to the subject adds a bit of interest.
	I do laminate this resource because I can move the resource around the classroom when highlighting points in lessons and re-use for following years.	Above the board, is a number line, provided by the school. For my maths board, I tend to keep a blank canvas as I prefer to use it to stick extension challenges and worked examples from lessons for pupils' reference. I also like to use it to stick my handwritten maths posters up to introduce a new topic or consolidate prior knowledge. Again, nothing fancy, just some flipchart pens, a ruler and brief explanation with models. For example, for an introductory poster on area, I would quickly write a definition of area and then draw some shapes showing that you can work

out area counting squares or using a formula for rectangles. This strategy is quite popular with elementary American teachers who call them anchor charts. If you're interested in seeing some examples, please type in 'anchor charts + subject' into your online search engine.

To make my glossary posters, I reach for my copy of Carol Vorderman's: *Help Your Kids with Maths: A Unique Step-by-Step Visual Guide*, which provides child-friendly explanations and saves time searching online.

I also use the website *CGP Plus* vocabulary cards for key topics as they provide mathematical definitions in a simple way. These vocabulary

			cards are a great way of quizzing pupils and getting them to use the Maths Working Wall, if they forget key terms. This is a resource that I paid for as I felt that it was worth the money, because I also use it for other subjects, too, as it features PowerPoints, worksheets and display materials.
3. SCIENCE			
Sensational Science		If I have time, I put some pictures related to the topic and then surround the photos with corresponding scientific vocabulary.	I use ready-made vocabulary cards from *CGP Plus* linked to the units under discussion.
4. WELLBEING AND PUPIL ADMIN			
Fire drill		In the event of a drill, line and move in silence. Numbered names of your pupils.	Hopefully, your school will provide you with a fire drill list but if not, make one and laminate it. I will share this resource in Chapter 5.

		Number of boys Number of girls This fire drill register needs to be laminated.	During morning registration, I fill it in with a whiteboard marker showing who is/are absent. At the end of the day, I clean it.
Locker numbers		As above but remove the fire-drill-related text and replace with 'Locker Numbers'.	To create this resource, just remove the fire-drill-related text. Once you have done this, print off and laminate, then write the locker number for each pupil by using a permanent black marker. It is useful to have this to make identifying pupils' lockers easier, just in case a pupil goes home ill, and they need their belongings. In some schools, you can simply label lockers with pupils' names.
Check-in signage		Depending on your school, you may need to implement a wellbeing system.	I made this is in Microsoft Word. Here it is:

	Then you can make some simple name tags in Microsoft Word and laminate them. These name tags are then placed by the level of how they are feeling (please see opposite).	**Feeling great!** **Okay** **Not so good** *Picture 20: Check in*
5Bs independence	You may have heard about the 5Bs already. It's a prompt to encourage independence because some pupils have learned helplessness. The 5Bs are: Brain Board Book Buddy Boss	I found a poster of the 5Bs on *Twinkl* but you could make your own.

	I don't laminate this resource. I just enlarge it in A3 and have it Blu-tacked to a wall near the front for ease of reference.	
SLANT	How we listen: use **SLANT** **S**it up straight **L**isten **A**nswer and ask questions **N**ever interrupt **T**rack the teacher	I like the simplicity of some of Doug Lemov's strategies in *Teach Like a Champion*, and SLANT is a well-publicised acronym in the world of education that I have adopted. I drill SLANT into my pupils from day one! This is a permanent fixture on my main whiteboard and is laminated.
T.H.I.N.K. poster	Poster content: *Before you speak* *THINK* T is it TRUE? H is it HELPFUL? I is it INSPIRING? N is it NECESSARY? K is it KIND?	I also teach my students the well-known acronym T.H.I.N.K. as shown opposite. There are several images of this online.

Focusing on one area at a time forces to you to pay attention to detail about what impacts learning.

Once you have printed off, laminated, cut, guillotined, etc., experiment with the placement of your display resources by dotting them around the classroom by securing with Blu-Tack first. When you are happy with the placement of your materials, you can staple securely at an angle. You must remember to staple at an angle because stapling flat makes the removal of staples incredibly difficult if you make a mistake or need to change your display boards.

As you can see from the above, there is little personal artwork in sight and the images that I have in my bank of resources are from *Clipart* or other online images. It does take some time cutting out letters but because I have a bank of reliable, ready-to-go resources, I can just print off my display resources and immediately get on with the business of cutting, etc.

Corridor Display Boards

You may be called upon to change corridor displays on a termly or half-termly basis, and it is expected by most schools that the corridor displays have a bit more 'wow' factor. If you do not have TA support, this can be hard to fit in along with your other teaching duties. If you don't have help in this regard, keep it as low-maintenance as possible. Below are some of the ways in which I create external display boards:

- Yellow is my favourite colour of choice; however, this is not always in supply, so I use blue or silver with black borders and lettering, as these colours are gentle on the eyes.
- I use Century Gothic again and try to avoid long titles, so I don't have to cut out as many letters.
- Parental authorisation permitting, I enlarge colour photographs of children at work to A4 to fill up the space.

- I ensure that the children's written work takes precedence, as the children and the work are true ambassadors of the school; let their work and smiley faces do the talking.
- I write a brief blurb about what the work is about.
- I back the blurb, written work, photos and name tags on black sugar paper and that's it.

If I have time, I will put some images related to the topic by trawling the internet. If I am on a roll, I will make some 3D images; for example, for a textile display I prepared, I made a huge needle from foil and then thread through some black ribbon through the eye of the needle. I then attached the ribbon to a large cotton reel that I made from an empty kitchen towel roll and two card circles (one glued at each end) and then wound some black tissue paper around the empty kitchen roll to make it look like a full reel.

When all is said and done, if your pupils are learning, feel safe and happy in your classroom and know that they are loved and cared for, they won't care about your lack of display dazzle.

In a nutshell:

1. You don't need a showy, cluttered classroom for successful learning to happen, and do not be disheartened if you see colleagues with more decorative, elaborate classrooms than yours. **Don't fall into the trap of besting others. Instead, whittle down your materials to what you deem impactful.**

2. Understand that the classroom is for the children's learning; anything else is redundant and displays should not be wallpaper but rather **high-quality materials that are easily visible and promote learning.** You need to **filter out the waffle, let go of the excess** and be **selective.** Each display should be **referenced** and used by both you and your pupils. Make your classroom come alive through excellent examples of shared writing, keywords, punctuation definitions and vocabulary mind maps. Show children what

to avoid (banned words) in their written work and provide exemplification so they know the steps to success that they are working towards.

3. **Don't worry, be ready!** Before the commencement of the academic year, prepare and photocopy the materials for your display boards in advance so you don't have to go into school during the summer holidays. If you have a TA, they can support you with this. **More hands make light work.**

4. Remember to keep your working walls tidy by **removing out-of-date material.**

Drop Dazzling Displays!

Notes

Chapter 5
Awesome Organisation

I enjoy reading about the habits of successful people and one thing that they all have in common is that they have clear routines, with many of them starting their day at daybreak to maximise their productivity. I am a morning person, but I know I would be on my knees if I woke up at 5am every working day, which is why you must be true to yourself and know what works for you. I would love to be able to wake up early during term time, meditate and journal, head to the gym before work, but I know that I would not survive that kind of schedule during my working days; you have to start the day in the right way for you. Outlined in this chapter is the use of routines and templates to reduce workload and optimise learning. Not only do templates and routines free up teachers, but they also put pupils at ease, as they are able to think about content within a familiar framework rather than worrying about understanding what it is they are being asked to do. In a word, effective routines and organisation lead to automaticity.

Alarms

To avoid clock-watching, which stresses me out sometimes, I set the following alarms on my mobile phone, which I change as and when necessary:

Monday – Friday alarm:	06:00	Get up
Monday alarm:	08:20	Monday alarm for morning staff briefing
Monday – Friday alarm:	08:30	Back in the classroom, ready to receive pupils

| Monday – Friday alarm: | 13:00 | Nearing the end of lunch time |
| Monday – Friday alarm: | 17:15 | Head for home |

Setting alarms allows me to sustain my concentration and get into the flow of what I am doing without looking at my phone all the time. The last alarm is especially important as you do not want to upset the site manager and be metaphorically frogmarched off the property.

Before Work

The night before work, I have a ritual which involves checking the **weather forecast** and preparing my **work outfit** accordingly. I don't generally wear make-up but, if school photographs are due, I will apply simple make-up – lipstick gloss, blusher and mascara. I ensure that my **lunch bag** and **teaching resources** are ready for the day ahead, and that my breakfast has been poured into a bowl and covered in advance the night before. If rain is forecast at lunchtime, I will mentally plan ahead to ensure that I have the books that need to be marked in a bag, so I can make a quick exit at lunchtime and find a quiet space to mark. I always try to mark as many books as possible at lunchtime to minimise or halve the marking load after school.

Get Into a Work Routine

Ultimately, you will need to find out what works for you to set the tone for your teaching days. If you have children of your own, you may not be able to stay late at work and will need to adopt a different schedule. I prefer to wake up early and arrive at work early, as I find schools are quieter from 07:00–08:00. I regard this as my 'monastery hour', as I spend it in silence, setting up for the day and doing any **last-minute photocopying** that I may have forgotten; working through my **action list** in my diary; checking my morning **emails at 08:00** (not before, as I think it is important to set one's own agenda and not be disturbed first thing in the morning by someone else's agenda); and **marking** any remaining books that I did not have the chance to mark the day before.

***Important**: Upon entry to your classroom, ensure that your interactive whiteboard works, and that the internet is working. If there are any issues, you can hopefully have them resolved before the children arrive.

It is a good idea to **time yourself** when you're planning and marking to understand how long these two essential components of teaching take; by doing this, you'll be able to manage your time better.

Furthermore, take note of how you feel during these time slots; for example, what are your energy levels like? If you find yourself flagging at 15:30, you might wish to do something less taxing, such as photocopying, guillotining or writing lesson evaluations.

By analysing your effectiveness, you'll be able to prioritise the time of day that works best for you; for example, during my planning in the summer break, I get up at 05:30 because I am more alert in the early mornings and can watch the birds in the garden feeding; it's a beautiful, peaceful and quiet time to work. I only wake up at this time during my holidays, as I could not survive waking up this early during term time. Once you find your rhythm and groove, work life will become easier. I also **check the weather forecast** online so I can plan lessons during the holiday on cloudy wet days, and plan leisure activities for warm, bright days. That said, I do try to complete my planning in one stretch so I can square it away and properly relax and recuperate for the remainder of the holiday.

During Lessons

I strive to give feedback to pupils verbally and conduct live marking wherever possible to minimise my marking load outside of school hours, as evenings should be your own. More importantly, marking in this way also provides pupils with immediate feedback, which supports progress.

During Break

School days are full on; therefore, it is important to have a healthy snack during breaks. I try to remain hydrated, and I do like to munch on an apple or piece of fruit during break time as I find this keeps my level energy up.

During Lunch

Pupils pile their books with relevant pages open, which enables me to mark the books straight away without having to flick through them to find the work. My lunch hour is spent marking books for 45 minutes, and 15 minutes for lunch and a toilet visit, but this varies depending on the written outcomes produced on the day. If the morning has been a trying one, I will play some relaxing music (through *YouTube*) whilst marking; otherwise, I prefer to mark in silence.

Batch and Spread!

Where possible, to keep things simple, I try to organise days according to a subject or theme. Batching tasks a week in advance in this way enables me to spread them across the week, which makes workload more focused and manageable, as I am not constantly switching between tasks. Here is an example of what a weekly routine might look like:

Magical Monday: Photocopy spellings for the following week and guillotine.

Terrific Tuesday: Photocopy reading for the following week and guillotine.

Wonderful Wednesday: Photocopy maths and English for the following week and guillotine.

Tremendous Thursday: Photocopy geography/history for the following week and guillotine.

Fantastic Friday: Review and finalise resources for the week ahead and guillotine. (*'Late Friday' is usually a day when I have the photocopier to myself because everyone has departed, and I can blitz through any remaining photocopying).

Sensational Saturday: Free choice

Soulful Sunday: Visit the gym and batch cook for the week ahead. Chores – dust, vacuum, wash and put clothes away, and then rest of the day is off.

If you're unable to subject batch, just ensuring that you photocopy a day in advance will help to alleviate last-minute copying; for example, photocopy the following Monday's resources the previous Friday; and then photocopy Tuesday's resources on Monday, and so on.

Tips:

- Always go to the photocopier with your laptop in hand, just in case the item you sent to print did not materialise.
- To support with the planning of meals, and if you have cash to splurge, you may wish to subscribe to a meal recipe and delivery service. In the past, I was stuck in a rut on the culinary front and was thoroughly bored of my own cooking; therefore, I opted for this on a temporary basis to get my creative juices flowing again and kept the recipe cards for future use.

I have been fortunate to have worked with colleagues who willingly shared planning, guillotining and photocopying labour; therefore, I did not have to do as much on my own as shown in the example above. By batching according to subject, you can guillotine with greater ease and not muddle up resources. Batching resources also helps TAs if they are guillotining lots of paper across different classes.

Maximise PPA

There is far too much nonsense in education that takes up valuable time. Prioritising visible tasks, such as marking, planning and pastoral matters, are of paramount importance and these are the teaching commitments that count and must be remembered, even when faced with the 'style over substance' culture that has taken root in certain schools. I know that I prefer to plan at home as there are fewer distractions and, luckily for me, I currently work in a school that allows PPA to be done off-site, so planning can be completed then. At school, I do live marking in lessons and encourage my pupils to mark their own work where possible, particularly in maths. I also mark books during some of my lunchtime to reduce marking at home and ensure that I have photocopying and guillotining sorted. If you work in a two- or three-form entry school, this may not always be possible, as you have a duty to your immediate colleagues to work collaboratively to support priorities such as planning, data entry, moderating pupils' work, emails addressed to the year group, extra-curricular events, school productions, Maths Week, etc. However, if you've been working in the same school for a number of years and good planning is already in place, then this might free you up, so that you don't have to spend every day of the week working at home.

After School

I try to avoid bringing work home with me by staying at school until 5:00 or 5:30pm. I spend this time marking, photocopying and tweaking slides and resources in light of lesson evaluations.

By staying late on a Friday, when most staff have left early, I can get on top of any outstanding photocopying and guillotining. Working late on a Friday also means that I don't have to work during my weekend; I neutralise the resentment I would feel if I had to work during the weekends. The only instance when I work weekends is report writing season or class assemblies.

Keyboard Shortcuts

If you use *Microsoft Windows*, it is worthwhile familiarising yourself with its shortcuts. Please see https://www.computerhope.com/shortcut/word.htm.

Snipping Tool is a good Microsoft app to use. A former colleague of mine told me about it and I am forever grateful, as it saved me from having to print screen and crop each time that I wanted to copy an image or text.

Get Friendly with the Photocopier!

You can save some time and paper by familiarising yourself with the photocopier; for example, minimising A4 to A5, printing on both sides to save paper, etc. I used to reduce A4 to A5 so that I could have two A5 sheets together to form A4, and then I only had to produce fifteen copies instead of thirty for my class. If you're not sure how to use the different functions, ask someone from admin to show you. If the photocopier does not have this function, you can use the printer options for printing, which allows you to put more than one page per sheet. You can also change the sizing – A4, B5, etc.

Emails

I am showing my age here, but I remember a time in my teaching career before emails existed. I enjoyed this time before emails. Everyone had to be super organised and not change things at the drop of a hat in a disorganised manner. We did not have countless off-timetable events; and we talked and debated more effectively in team meetings and briefings. Although emails can be a blessing, they have become serious time thieves and have played a large part in killing the art of conversation.

Today, many organisations would not survive without email, especially with the prevalence of remote working, but I have found some ways to navigate emails by having some firm, non-negotiable routines in place, which I will now take you through.

Folders for Emails

When starting a new job, I organise emails into the following folders:

- SEND & Medical — In this folder, I place any information related to pupils' specific needs.
- Parents — Any messages or queries make their way into this folder.
- Pupil Admin — Any information related to computer access for school software, such as *Accelerated Reader, Times tables Rockstars, Spelling Bee, Education City*, etc.
- IT — Information related to my school access details, such as photocopying access, school-related sites such as Arbor or SIMS goes here.
- School templates — Planning overviews, school calendars, newsletters.

Checking Emails

Don't continually check emails and mute notifications so that you do not hear them coming in, as the pinging is distracting. I keep on top of emails by **deleting** as appropriate and ensuring that I act on emails at **daily set times of my choosing,** not as and when they arrive, and I endeavour to respond to emails within 24 hours. Reduce your screen time by checking at set intervals instead; for example: 08:00, 12:00 (lunch time); and before 17:00. I **pin** or **red flag** important emails to the top and leave emails unread until I have responded to them. I make it a rule not to check emails after 17:00 and when sick, I do not check emails at all. If you find yourself on medical leave, set up an auto-responder message to make it clear to all that you are recuperating, not working. Example:

> Dear X,
>
> Thank you for your email. I am now unavailable until <u>Tuesday X December X</u>. I will respond to your message upon my return.
>
> Kind regards,
>
> *Signature*
>
> Teacher
>
> Name of school
>
> School logo

You do not need to provide a reason because not everyone who emails needs to know about your health, as this is personal information.

There are some teachers who read emails during quiet lesson moments, but I **never read emails during lessons** now because any negative emails read can have an adverse impact on the rest of your day, and you certainly don't want to have to contend with the additional strain of emotionally unsettling emails coupled with teaching a mixed-ability class of thirty pupils.

Email Notifications on Your Mobile

Personally, I do not have professional email apps installed on my phone as I don't wish to be disturbed outside of working hours. **Life comes before work.** In my opinion, the only time you should have email notifications on your phone is for your own personal emails or if you run your own company. If you must have an email app installed on your phone, it is good idea to apply 'Do not disturb' settings from 17:00–07:00; otherwise, you might hear or see notifications during your sleeping hours.

Email Copy

Some of the email content that I write is repetitive in nature, which means that I can use the same wording with a few adjustments. Firstly, I make a template of this by saving as a draft email (the 'Drafts Folder' is where I keep all my email templates). Next, I copy the text from the draft and paste it into a new email. I keep my emails short and sweet – don't write lots of text as no-one enjoys reading voluminous emails. Here is an example of a typical email:

Line: Year X's Newsletter + date
Dear X,
Please find attached a copy of **name of year X's/class** newsletter.
Kind regards,
Signature
Teacher
Name of school
School logo

This email example is formal, short and to the point. Always punctuate your emails properly, be professional and don't be tempted to use excessive punctuation, such as exclamation and question marks, as this can give readers the wrong impression of you and create panic. When drafting emails, you may wish to write the body of your email in *Microsoft Word* first for **proofreading** purposes, as some email providers do not highlight misspellings and grammar. If you wish to use emojis, only use for your immediate colleagues, such as those in your year team, or those you regard as friends.

I sign off each email with a ready-made **email signature** (use the 'Help' function in your email provider to help you set this up), which is much quicker than typing my name each time I craft an email. I follow the school's email format, such as logo (if applicable) and school contact details.

A **subject line** needs to be to the point as it helps your colleagues to determine whether it applies to them or not; however, staff should not, as a rule, send blanket emails to all staff unless it's meant for *all* staff, as this just wastes valuable time. One school in which I worked had a system in place that prevented the emailing of blanket emails, and I truly appreciated this as it stopped my inbox from becoming thoroughly congested. If you needed to send a whole school email, you had to forward to SLT; otherwise, you had to step up a gear and take the time to enter the addresses of the relevant people.

Be kind and don't be passive aggressive by celebrating individuals in a global email in a veiled attempt to shame and spur others into action, as this will never be well received. By way of example, here is a typical scenario:

> Dear All,
>
> Firstly, a huge thank you and well done to A, B and C for adhering to the Spring data deadline; however, those of you who have yet to provide data, it is imperative that this be forwarded to me by 17:00 today.

Although this email may not appear ostensibly particularly bothersome or threatening in tone, individuals named and celebrated will not enjoy being on the receiving end of potentially jealous colleagues, and those shamed (i.e. those not named) will feel miffed and belittled. If you wish to celebrate staff, do so in a wholly positive manner which does not involve condemning others. If you need to contact individuals who are failing to live up to expectations or deadlines, speak to them or email them directly, as there may be legitimate reasons for their failure to meet a deadline.

If you find yourself in a position where these kinds of emails are the norm, don't sweat it! Instead, be as positive as you possibly can be and bear in mind not to compose emails of this nature yourself.

Carbon Copying

On another note, avoid carbon copying everyone into emails unless it directly applies to them; for example, organising a school trip and keeping all those involved in the loop merits the carbon copying. Copying others into emails because you are experiencing trouble with specific colleagues can be perceived as passive aggressive; for example, a middle manager having a problem with an ECT not planning lessons and cc'ing the headteacher in the first instance could be perceived as passive aggressive, especially if this is the first time the ECT has been notified of their wrongdoing.

Carbon copying has its use but if you persistently misuse it to be passive aggressive or to cover your backside, this will dilute the power of your message. What is more, if you come to be viewed as a serial copier (a CC'er), your message will likely be ignored by all, which defeats the purpose.

Top Tips:

- If you are not sure how or where to begin with the composition of emails, you may find Chat GPT a useful starting point.
- Avoid 'Replying to All' unless your response does truly apply to all the recipients.
- Don't send snotty and snooty emails as no-one will appreciate those kinds of messages!

Electronic Bookmarks & Pinning

If you regularly use certain internet sites as part of your teaching, ensure that you bookmark them for ease of reference; for example, I have *'I LOVE PDF'* as a bookmark because I use it when converting PDFs to PowerPoints and vice versa. I also bookmark *Topmarks* for maths games, *Newsround,* which I use as a settler either after lunch or at home time, and some Christmas songs from *YouTube* are also bookmarked. If you or your school are willing to pay, you can stop the ads popping up.

For convenience, I pin my lesson planning folder and behaviour folder to the bottom of my computer screen so that I do not have to browse the computer for these regularly used files. I also sometimes use the 'Quick Access' function in *Microsoft*.

Reading Records

Reading is a vital life skill. I read as much as I can to my pupils to promote a love of reading and provide ample opportunities for them to read during school hours, such as upon entry, reading my slides, after lunch and at the end of the day. I also expect parents/carers to play their role in supporting good reading habits and, with TA assistance, I will routinely check that pupils are reading at least three times a week at home by checking their Reading Records. Pupils who read regularly are awarded with house points.

Laptop Usage

If you are lucky enough to have an in-situ computer and laptop, you can keep track of remaining slides by referring to the laptop during lessons, reminding yourself of what's coming up next and which slides to skip, if needs must. You can also readily refer to the answer scheme embedded in your slides and call out answers verbally rather than accidentally sharing answers prematurely because you have forgotten to freeze the screen. This routine helps me to stay on track and ensure that lessons run smoothly.

Christmas Resources

I routinely roll out the same resources every year – a Christmas decoration-making activity that consists of a piece of plain paper and a pair of scissors (easy to resource); photocopies of blank Christmas bookmarks on card for pupils to colour in; and a range of festive coloured card as well as basic Christmas-themed shapes (borrowed from a teacher-friend), such as Christmas trees to make Christmas cards. Pupils cut out the Christmas shapes and stick onto the card. Afterwards, they can add sequins for added sparkle. For those who wish to make their own card without templates, they are free to do so. This routine takes out the stress of having to think what to do every year. For reasons of copyright, I am unable to include images of the resources used here but with a little bit of research, I'm sure that you will find some.

Electronic Folder Organisation

For the organisation of electronic files, I have the core subjects at the top and I number the lesson folders. If you prefer, you could list your subjects in alphabetical order:

1. Early work
2. English
3. Reading
4. Spellings
5. Handwriting
6. Maths
7. Science
8. History
9. Geography
10. Art
11. DT
12. Spanish/French
13. PE
14. RE
15. Computing
16. Homework
17. PSHE
18. Music
19. Wellbeing Weds

Assembly
Cover
Materials
Off timetable
Other Teaching
Templates

I then subdivide the subject folders according to term for ease of reference, with topics organised according to week of the academic year; for example: Week 1 Poetry, Week 2 Poetry, etc.

If you use **Google Drive**, you have the option to **colour-code** folders, which is useful if you're a visual person.

Top Tips:
- Try to keep file names short as long file names can make backing up files difficult. In the past, I lost many files when I transferred data to a new computer because my file name extensions were too long; for example, *Microsoft Windows* currently has a maximum of 256 characters.

- If you want to organise your folders chronologically, you could add the date to your named file by prefacing named files with a date, for example:

  01.08.24 Wk 1 Poetry

  08.08.24 Wk 2 Poetry

- To ensure that my planning folder is right at the top, I use an underscore to preface the name of the file like this:

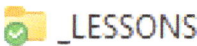 _LESSONS

For files that I wish to relegate to the bottom, I preface with a z underscore as shown below:

z_MISCEL SCH

- Remember you can toggle through the files by using the 'Sort' function which allows you to sort by name, date modified, type of file, ascending and descending.

Templates

Templates are a great way of reducing workload. You do have to invest time in making them but once they're there, you're good to go! To avoid decision fatigue, I tend to stick to the **same colour scheme** and **font style**, as well as the same **line thickness** for boxes and tables. I like to think of my templates as my brand. Whatever theme you decide to choose, stick to it, as it is another way to automate your practice.

Here are some examples of templates I use in my teaching practice:

- Cover plan (Appendix 1)
- Medical proforma (Appendix 2)
- Supply teacher handover template (Appendix 3)
- Weekly timetable (Appendix 4)

- Weekly overview (Appendix 5) – I used this template at the start of my primary teaching career when all things primary were new to me. I find that having one side of A4 forces me to be concise.
- For class blogs, I use a *Microsoft* Newspaper template which I adapt. You can go online and find different free templates to choose from.
- If my school does not provide a calendar for the year, I use the free site *Calendarpedia* as it provides a range of calendars in Word, Excel and PDF. https://www.calendarpedia.co.uk/
- PE template (Appendix 6)
- Photocopying template (Appendix 7) – I laminate on pink paper so that it stands out. I tick the appropriate circle next to the options so that TAs know what is required in the way of photocopying.
- If you have several adults working with you, I recommend that you use this overview, so all staff know what the learning objectives are. (Appendix 8)
- Behaviour reflection template which I sourced from *Twinkl*.
- Whole-class marking template from my school which, for reasons of copyright, I cannot include here but there are many templates available online.

PowerPoint Templates

One of the ways in which I reduce my lesson planning workload is to use PowerPoint templates. I have made my own templates and experimented with many different types of teaching slides over the years, but have found that adapting the free *Microsoft PowerPoint* **Jacquetta** template works best for me because it looks tidy, clean and bold. If your school uses Google Slides or SMART Notebook, these ideas can still be applied. I prefer to use PowerPoint now because PowerPoint is used by many organisations and, during lockdown, PowerPoint was more accessible to the masses whereas SMART Notebook was not readily available.

If *Microsoft PowerPoint* templates do not float your boat, you could create your own. There are also other PowerPoint template sites, such as *Canva* but you must create an account, and not all slide presentations are free of charge.

By way of example, here is a step-by-step guide to my PowerPoint template:

Step 1: Below is my **graphics page** which is the first page of my PowerPoint template. You may have noticed that the slide page is numbered; this is deliberate as I use page numbers to help stay on track with my time management. This page contains my favourite online pictures/symbols that I recycle in my lesson presentations. Having all my frequently used graphics in one place makes locating them much easier.

Picture 21: Graphics Page

Step 2: The next slide features **subject badges, which I add to the title page of different PowerPoints according to subject**. If I have many PowerPoints open, the subject badges make it immediately apparent which slideshow I need to open at various points of the day. You may wish to **colour-code subjects** to make distinguishing between slideshows even easier; for example, you could have a light blue background for maths; light green for science, and so on. Currently, I don't do this as I use a cream-coloured background for my slides to support dyslexic pupils.

Picture 22: Subject Badges

Step 3: Following on from this, I include a **contents page with hyperlinks** dedicated to individual lessons. When I plan PowerPoints for English units, I create one master PowerPoint for the entire unit as it means that I can refer to previous learning with ease, but the problem with this is that you can have up to 100 plus pages within a presentation, which is where the hyperlinks come in handy. By having a contents page, each lesson can be easily navigated.

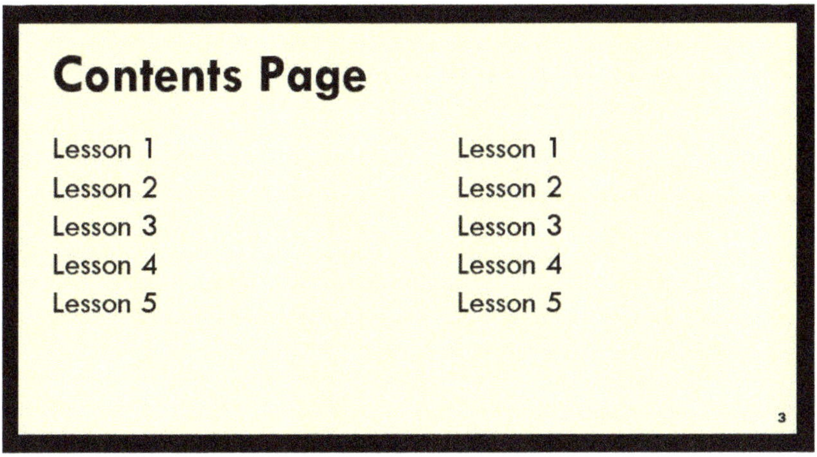

Contents Page

Lesson 1   Lesson 1
Lesson 2   Lesson 2
Lesson 3   Lesson 3
Lesson 4   Lesson 4
Lesson 5   Lesson 5

Picture 23: Hyperlinked Contents Page

Hyperlinking Tips: Highlight 'Lesson 1' text, then right click on 'Link' and select 'Place in This Document' option. Repeat this process for each lesson.

Step 4: Next is a **lesson summary**. Here is a blank template of the lesson summary. I don't always include this but if I am sharing my resources with colleagues, I will insert this lesson summary as a quick overview to help them and the students understand the rationale behind the activities and provide quick instruction. If you work in a prescriptive school that demands detailed lesson plans, you can leave this slide out.

Lesson 1 Summary		
Activity	Description	Time
1		

Picture 24: Lesson Summary

Step 5: For slideshows which require more than my usual type of resourcing, I use this **Teacher Resources** page so that I know at a glance what needs to be printed or photocopied.

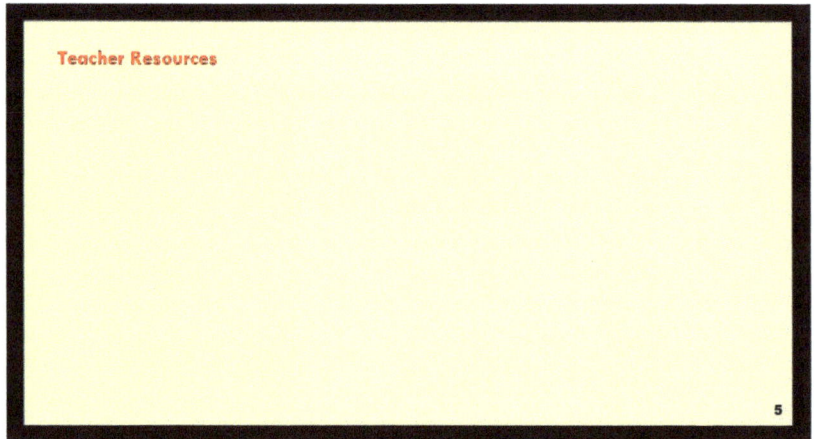

Picture 25: Teacher Resources

Step 6: Next is a **title page, which is where I insert the subject badge.** When I plan individual lessons for each lesson, I colour-code the lettering, which in this case is Lesson 1: Personification, using the colours of the rainbow: red for lesson 1; orange for lesson 2; yellow for lesson 3; green for lesson 4; and blue for lesson 5.

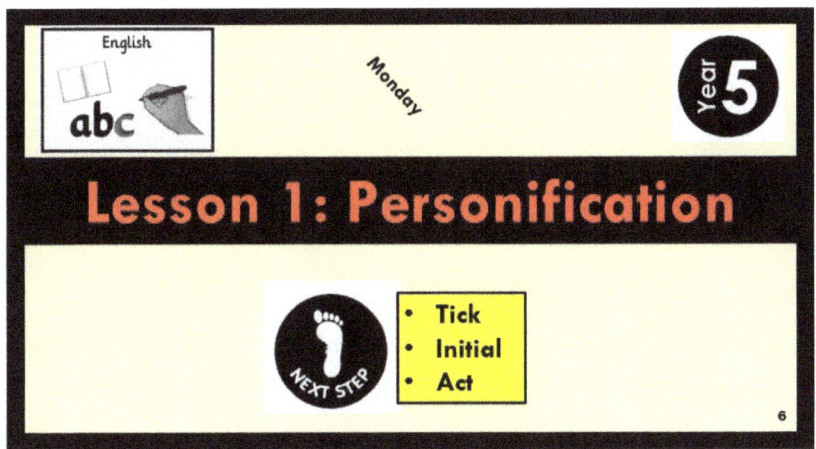

Picture 26: Title Page

Step 7: This '**What You Need**' slide is something that I borrowed from the teaching website *Oak Academy* during lockdown. It serves as a gentle reminder for pupils who may have absent-mindedly forgotten their equipment at the start of the lesson. Not all classes need this kind of reminder; therefore, you could delete this slide if you want. At the start of the year, I ensure that I model book presentation, such as using a ruler to draw a margin in maths books, underlining dates, titles and learning objectives under the visualiser; therefore, this means that pupils will only need basic equipment anyway.

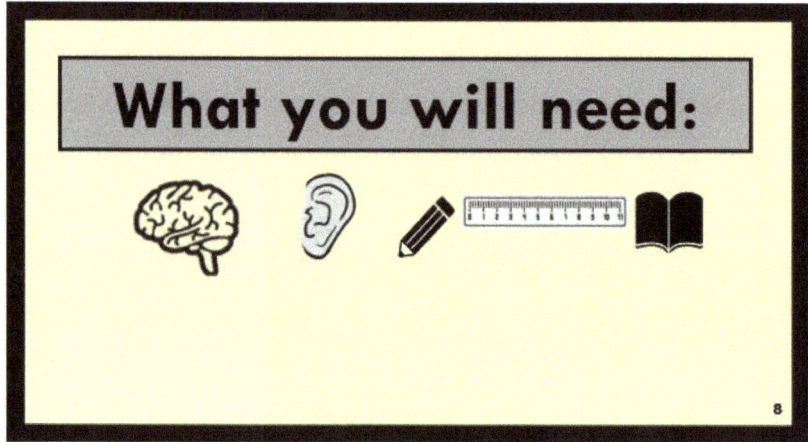

Picture 27: Equipment

Step 8: The **starter and what I expect children to learn** slide. I set the Learning Objective (L.O.) and differentiated Success Criteria (S.C.) against a yellow backdrop to make it explicit to children what I expect them to accomplish, how this will be achieved and why they are learning this topic.

L.O.: To identify personification in a range of poems.
S.C.:
❑ Identify examples of personification.
❑ Complete personification sentences.
❑ Write own examples of personification.

In English, for example, I tend to start every lesson with a differentiated high-quality SPaG task which links to the subsequent lesson. I cycle through the same kind of tasks throughout the year. Using repeated tasks means that pupils immediately understand what they need to do instead of having to have the instructions explained to them. I discuss this in more detail in Chapter 8.

On this slide and subsequent slides, I have inserted a tab on the right-hand side that signposts the lesson number currently being studied. Again, these colour-coded tabs are in the sequence of the rainbow. **Each slide features the L.O.** as I want the aim of the lesson to be clear to my pupils, and anyone who walks in the classroom will also be able to clearly see what the lesson is about. There are occasions when I will delete the lesson tabs; for example, if the slideshow is long and I'm short on time, or if the tabs interfere with text or images that I have inserted.

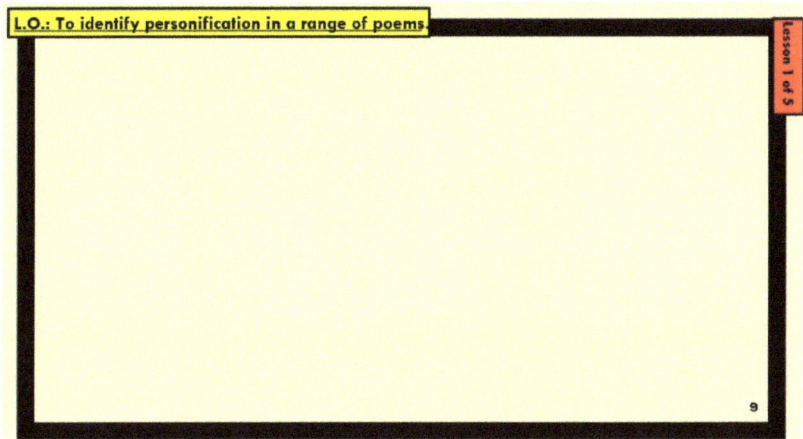

Picture 28: Coloured Tab

Additional slides are inserted as necessary, including models and vocabulary vault slides, discussion slides, shared write and task slides. I try not to have too much text on each slide (no more than five bullet points), and I prefer to deliver verbal instruction in conjunction with **visuals** to keep content memorable. I don't want pupils trying to read dense text from the PowerPoint whilst I am speaking, as this splits their attention. If you do need to list more than five points, number them instead and animate each bullet point one at a time whilst addressing each point verbally; this staggered approach supports pupils' focus. For all these additional slides, symbols are inserted rather than text to reduce clutter and to make it immediately clear to pupils what is expected of them.

Examples of symbols:

- Flower – symbolises 'extension, opportunities for growth, and "stretch-it" challenges.'
- Eye or magnifying glass – examples to read, visualisation
- Speech bubble – talk partner/discussion work
- Magpie image – vocabulary vault for Shared Writing
- Whiteboard symbol – signals pupils to take out their whiteboards.

Step 9: Nearing the end of my PowerPoint presentation, I include the following slides:

- Answers/editing slide templates
- Independent Task slide

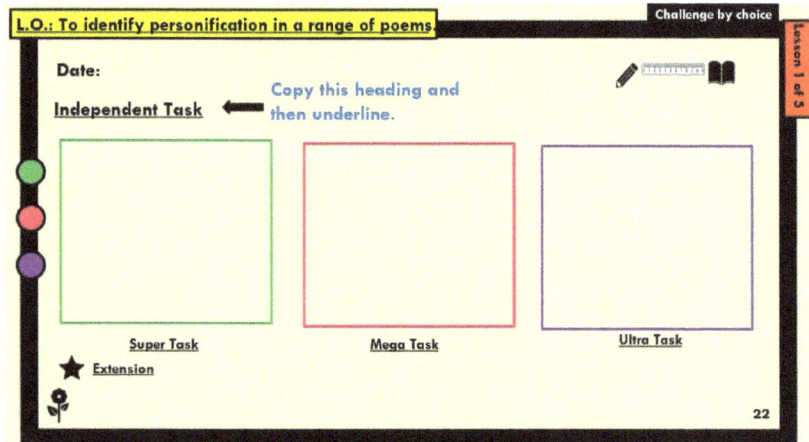

Picture 29: Independent Task Slide

- Celebration of Success

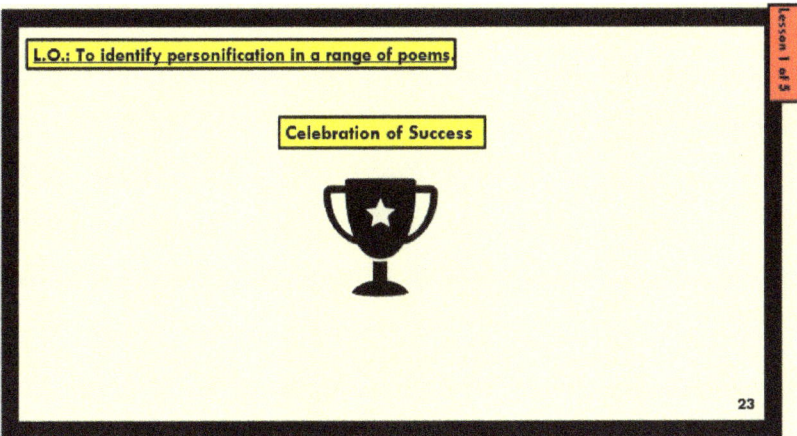

Picture 30: Celebration of Success

- Plenary
- Evaluation – pupils rate their learning on their learning sticker by circling R, A or G, or colour in the letter 'O' of the L.O. if they have written the learning objective by hand. Here is the evaluation slide that I use:

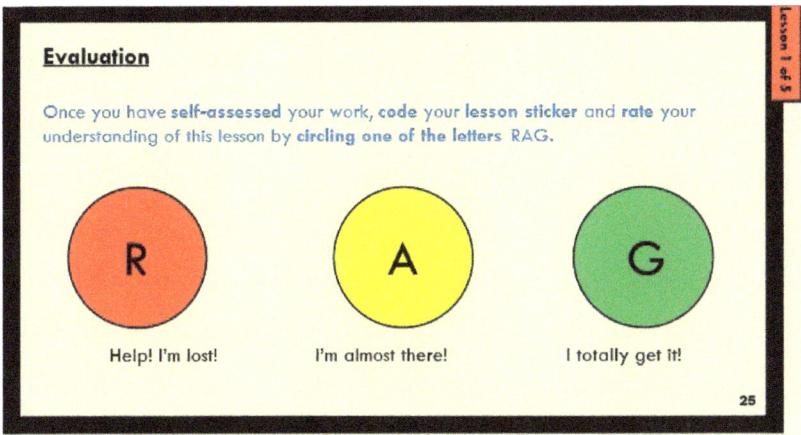

Picture 31: Evaluation

Step 10: Once I have finished creating my lesson PowerPoints, I delete the template slides I no longer need, such as the graphics page, subject badges, etc.

I use the Snipping Tool app to take screenshots of text and images. The shortcut for this is Windows logo key + Shift + S.

When using the template to create a lesson, I override my template master file by saving it as a different file name; for example: Week 1 Poetry. This way, I don't accidentally mess up my master template. It is important to save as you go along to avoid data loss due to technical issues.

Top Tip: If you are not familiar with PowerPoint, there are plenty of step-by-step *YouTube* videos available with time-saving hacks. Other video sharing sites are available!

Life Admin

Sometimes I feel like a slave to the kitchen. I enjoy cooking when I'm in the mood and have the time but when I have deadlines to meet, the last thing I need is to be making meals from scratch every single day; therefore, I sometimes do a meal preparation early in the morning on a Sunday. I make enough food to ensure that I have some left over for lunches.

Recently, I embraced a recipe box delivery service to add a bit of variety to my cooking repertoire, as I was stuck in a rut and wanted to try different recipes without the fuss. You can pause the service as and when you wish.

Apart from washing up, making the bed, cleaning the bathroom, maintaining a clean kitchen and emptying and taking out the bins, I don't do any chores during the working week. If I am up to it, I sometimes do my chores on a Friday evening, so that I have the entire weekend free, but this does not happen often. On Saturdays, I do what takes my fancy, and on Sundays, I do batch cooking (my husband also helps by cooking and preparing meals, which lightens the load), dusting, vacuuming, steaming floors (fortnightly), bleaching toilets, laundry, polishing shoes (weekly), watering the plants, and visiting the gym and supermarket (weekly/fortnightly). My favourite supermarket is close to the gym, which makes things super convenient. If you're pushed for time when it comes to grocery shopping, you could try internet shopping. I did this for a family member who was unwell and found it helpful; however, I do prefer to pick my own fruit and vegetables and will seek the items with the longest shelf life whereas with the internet shop, sometimes the fresh food selected was nearing expiry. Vacuuming is the first thing that doesn't get done if I am exhausted, closely followed by gardening and ironing (which are my least favourite chores). When I buy clothes, I will always seek clothing that is easy to iron or does not need ironing, as I am not a fan of ironing.

In short, I do the essentials (cleaning bathroom, kitchen and washing clothes) as a priority, as I'd much rather be out and about, having a roast dinner somewhere nice, visiting a gardening centre, coffee shop or going to the seaside on a fine day. Life is too short to be worrying about chores!

Top Tips:

- Invest in a cordless vacuum cleaner for a 'lick and a promise' clean. I'll quickly take out my cordless vacuum cleaner to stay on top of surface cleaning and use my Henry vacuum cleaner for a deep clean (other vacuum cleaners are available).
- If you live with family or others, suggest that they help with chores as more hands make light work!
- Stay on top of your finances by getting on board with internet banking, as you don't want to spend your Saturday mornings sorting out your finances.
- Use your holidays to arrange routine dental and eye appointments, holiday bookings, car MOT, and house and car insurance. During the holidays, I do my due diligence and use this time to look for alternative insurance providers to secure the best deals. This means that you won't fear a lapse

in your insurance and feel forced into paying for potentially expensive renewals with your current provider. Of course, it may be that your renewal dates do not coincide with school breaks but wherever possible, try to do this rather than having to squeeze in life admin during your working hours.

In a nutshell:

1. **Relish routine!** Organisation of your lesson resources saves you time, as you'll be able to find what you need at the click of a finger.
2. Well-thought-out **templates** are handy and save time.
3. Sharply focused, **high-value procedural starter tasks** promote independent working and consolidate knowledge.

Awesome Organisation

Notes

Chapter 6
Smarter Marking

Marking is for many teachers the bane of their lives and, to some extent, the autonomy you have in this regard will depend on the school's marking policy; for example, I once worked in a school which required green pen for 'growth' and pink for 'success'; it was time-consuming flitting between two different coloured pens. In recent years, there has been a move towards making marking less onerous for teachers and this is to be celebrated. Marking is a partnership between pupil and teacher and can be an effective way for pupils to improve their work and increase their knowledge, but it should not be exhausting. Furthermore, marking should not prevent teachers from having a life outside of school as this is unreasonable; I want you to have a life outside of work which includes full weekends to yourself. In this chapter, I will try to distil the best of what I have learned about managing marking.

Proofreading Symbols

I have been an advocate of **secretarial** codes for some time as they are **efficient** and **less labour-intensive**. Teaching pupils proofreading skills as part of an introductory English lesson is the best way to instil proofreading techniques whilst simultaneously teaching pupils proofreading symbols. Once pupils have learned this, marking is much easier. Just ensure that any new symbols you provide are the same or an addition to the school's marking policy, not a replacement.

Try to avoid writing reams and reams of feedback as your pupils will lose interest; instead, be succinct and **focus on the positives** wherever possible. For example, you could focus on one or two recurrent errors rather than all of them. Do not overdo the secretarial codes either, as this can produce too much visual clutter which makes it difficult for the pupils to read and improve on their work.

Here is a list of symbols that I use:

CL = capital letters

_ = lower case letter

P = punctuation

Sp = spellings

^ = missing information

↑ = Up-level/improve

g = grammar

~?~ = Sentence sense

// = new paragraph

= space

/ = eliminate

There are also **whole-class feedback templates** online which you can use whilst you are marking your pupils' books to record common misspellings, misconceptions, etc.; in fact, many schools are adopting this method over detailed teacher marking. I have used it in schools that implemented this system and found it useful, as I could record 'celebration and correction' as well as misconceptions that needed to be addressed easily. If I noticed that the same or similar errors were occurring for numerous pupils, I would type up the errors into a PowerPoint slide to feedback to the class at the beginning of the following lesson. Before officially beginning the lesson, I would display this feedback slide and elicit from pupils what they noticed before dissecting it as a class. This was helpful for pupils as it meant that the repetition of mistakes in subsequent lessons was avoided.

Live Marking

I circulate the classroom as much as possible once pupils are engrossed in an independent task in order to listen to them and provide verbal feedback. By discussing work with your pupils and marking during lessons, they will receive timely, meaningful feedback and you will avoid spending hours of marking after school. During lessons, I walk around the classroom with my **own whiteboard** and **marking pen** to support pupils with spellings, mathematical workings out, and the generation of ideas. I also have a **verbal feedback** stamp which I use when circulating my classroom.

When marking **text-rich** work, I use a Frixion pen, as this allows me to erase any accidental errors I might make when marking books.

Self and Peer Assessment

For maths, I use **check-it stations** (a table with answers on), which allow pupils to check their work against a mark scheme. They use editing pens to '**tick or fix**' their work. You will need to check that pupils are showing their workings where applicable and that these mathematical workings correspond with the answers. Once pupils can honestly mark their work, this approach can halve your marking time. If your class does not have the self-discipline to self-assess in this way, you could scan or record answers into your slideshow in advance or share answers under your visualiser.

If you have a class that is sensitive to the needs of others, you could get pupils to swap and **peer-assess** instead of self-assessing all the time. This works best with classes that have a good rapport. This does require training pupils in employing specific language of critique and the use of genre rubrics/success criteria, so that pupils can provide precise feedback.

High-quality Language

Encourage pupils to improve their language choices by avoiding 'banned words' (please see **Chapter 4** for further information on banned words). By teaching pupils to have thesaurus-thinking, they will learn to generate their own synonym suggestions. Providing word banks with genre-specific sentence types also supports pupils' writing. In your role as a teacher, it is also important to model excellent oratory skills by being fluent, avoiding multiple fillers, such as 'erm' and 'like', and employing good vocabulary. If you do this as standard, pupils will absorb your high expectations for speech and the written word, which will improve sentence structure. High-quality written work will, in turn, reduce your marking time as you will not have to spend an interminably long time trying to decipher sentences.

More recently, some schools are following the work of *Voice 21*, which is a national charity that supports schools to build speaking and listening in the curriculum[1]. If you work in a school which champions oracy, it may be easier to fulfil this aspect of teaching.

Open Books

At the end of the lesson, I instruct pupils to leave their books open for the lesson completed. This means that I do not need to flick through several pages to find the work requiring marking. I also instruct book monitors to collect them in table group order as this makes returning books easier for the following morning. I prefer to do my marking at school, even if that means staying late because I don't like carrying heavy books to the car. If you prefer to leave school early and take your books home with you, make certain that you do not mark in front of the television or have your mobile phone in front of you. If you need a bit of background noise, why not try listening to the radio instead, as this may be less distracting for you.

Sticky Index Tabs Page Markers

This is an approach I learned in a previous place of work and still use to this day. It is a useful way of highlighting specific areas that need extra work for pupils who frequently skip your comments and marking. Pupils respond to teacher feedback during Next Steps/ Dedicated Improvement Reflection Time (DIRT) and tick and initial the tab when they have acted on feedback. This way, when the books are collected, you can quickly check the tab and remove it if the pupil has successfully acted on feedback.

Precise Learning Objectives and Success Criteria

This could take the form of a sticker which could be ticked or highlighted in different colours according to the individual's success and your school's marking policy. This is particularly useful in lessons which do not require detailed marking. Success criteria serve as clear reference points which support pupils in taking responsibility for closely monitoring and self-assessing their own work. When pupils have a shared understanding of the success criteria, it means they have the ingredients to hand to be successful and are not stabbing in the dark.

Ron Berger's mantra **'kind, specific, helpful'** is something to bear in mind when explaining to pupils the importance of detailed feedback. I train my pupils in this 'kind, specific, helpful' approach (which is a variation of the 'Two Stars and a Wish' peer-assessment method). It is a great way of training pupils in providing constructive feedback. Peer assessors (or 'quality controllers' as I sometimes say to my pupils) record their feedback on Post-it notes, which takes the stress out of worrying about pupils writing in someone else's book. This could be done as a paired activity or a carousel activity, which involves pupils going from table to table with Post-it notes to look at the work of their peers. The carousel approach means that pupils return to their tables with a wide selection of detailed, high-quality feedback (much more than I could provide).

Kind

- I really like the way you_____
- Excellent _____ throughout
- The most successful thing about this was_____
- I enjoyed reading this because _____
- It was especially good when you_____

Specific

- In the first/second/third paragraph…
- I think _____ is quite difficult to understand/could be explained better/could include more detail etc
- Your sentence/paragraph about _____ was _____ because_____

Helpful (refer to success criteria)

- Think about adding a _____
- Think about taking away_____
- Have you thought about _____?
- To improve your _____ try_____
- Perhaps you could…

Picture 32: Kind, Specific, Helpful Feedback from Andrew Tharby's https://reflectingenglish.wordpress.com/author/atharby/page/8/[2]

Initially, this **'kind, specific, helpful'** strategy could be practised through whole-class constructive discussion; for example, at the start of some lessons (with the pupil's permission) I sometimes have a typed or photographed successful piece of work from one of the pupils, and I guide the class on why the pupil has matched the success criteria by using detailed feedback based on the stems above. If I don't have time to scan pupils' work into my PowerPoint or type up examples of pupil work, I can place it under my visualiser; I call this section of the lesson **'Celebration of Success'** but you could call it anything you like as long as it's celebratory, such as **'Star Writer'** or **'Hall of Fame'**.

Conversely, you could have an anonymous or fictional piece of writing which does not fully address the success criteria and direct the class to improve the piece, eliciting feedback from them on how best to edit the work.

Assessment

When marking lengthy assessments, such as mock SATs papers, I do not mark one paper in its entirety at a time; instead, I mark page 1 of each paper consecutively and pile it up, and then I repeat the process for page 2, etc. I find this much quicker than marking each paper in full, because the brain remembers the mark scheme when marking one page at a time and you'll find that you won't need to refer to the mark scheme as often.

For formal assessments, I also ensure that I input the results into a **single** *Excel* spreadsheet file. I use **one** *Excel* spreadsheet file because this allows me to switch easily between different subjects rather than opening individual assessment files for each. I simply create coloured tabs for each subject and click accordingly when inputting results. Also, using *Excel* means that percentages and score averages can be worked out automatically at the touch of a button rather than having to work out the results manually.

Homework

Gone are the days when I would painstakingly mark each piece of homework. Nowadays, I provide a short piece of homework that revises recent learning and can be self-marked. The work provided is work that pupils should be able to complete without assistance from parents. For pupils less fluent in maths, I will provide a differentiated homework task. I alternate between English and maths and always provide homework which contains models and worked examples to ensure a high success rate. I set the homework on Friday and go through the instructions, modelling some examples so pupils are more confident about what they need to do, which is then due on the following Friday. On Friday, my TA collects the homework books to check who has completed the homework, and those who have not completed the homework stay in at break to complete it. After break time, pupils self-assess their homework, and then new homework is distributed, and the cycle begins again.

The school in which you work may have a different way of setting homework; some schools now use IT-based homework for which pupils can provide instant feedback at the end, which means teachers do not have to mark homework; however, if your school expects teachers to do paper-based homework then I would stick to homework which consolidates prior learning, has a straightforward answer scheme, and does not cause undue stress in the home. Enrichment projects are lovely but if they require parents to source materials, etc., this can intrude on family time which, in turn, creates school resentment.

Stamps & Stickers

Hopefully, you're in a school that is fine with stamps and stickers; however, if you're in a school that is not keen, then this section won't apply. I use stamps as part of my marking process as they can be motivating. When marking, I have positive stamps and highlighters on the right-hand side and the improve/'even better if' stamps to my left. I use the inside of a tin lid or a piece of paper to stop inadvertent leakage on tables.

My favourite stamps (please see Chapter 1 for pictures):

Golden star – I use this to represent a merit/house point. I award this for a great effort or great work. For truly exceptional work, which goes above and beyond the success criteria, I insert a sparkly sticker.

- **Excellent** – I often will place this next to the star stamp.
- **Good** – If the work is of a good standard.
- **Verbal feedback** – If the school where I work insists on recording feedback.
- **Show your working** – Useful for maths work.

- **Underline** – Great for pupils who repeatedly forget to underline their learning objectives, dates and titles.
- **Next step** – Following on from this stamp, I write down specific pointers to move the pupil forward in his/her work. This stamp cuts down having to write 'Next step' in each book. You can get this stamp in different colours (purple, blue, green).

Focus on a maximum of three areas of improvement; otherwise, the pupil is likely to be disheartened. That said, I don't use this stamp very often as the **secretarial codes**, in the main, give pupils areas to improve. Some schools, particularly secondary schools, use numbered comment banks such as those listed below:

1. means > Include precise adjectives.
2. means > Add exciting verbs.
3. means > Vary your synonyms for 'said'.

If you work in a school which has a numbered comment bank stuck in the pupils' books, you will simply write the relevant number, and pupils could refer to the comment bank in their books to address what they need to do.

Numbering Books

At the beginning of the year, I instruct pupils to number their books according to their alphabetical place in the register. This is useful when having to complete detailed assessment reports on a database, as I can quickly organise the pupils' books in alphabetical order and work my way down the register.

Sampling

For ease of moderation purposes and book looks, I advise that you place coloured dots on the front of certain exercise books (about eight), so you know at a glance your: *Greater Depth, Expected, Working At,* and *Working Towards* children. I mark my dotted books first to get a feel for how successful the learning outcomes were. This sample approach gives me a generic indicator of how well new knowledge was applied during the lesson. Also, if a member of staff requests a sample of books at a moment's notice across the ability range, then I can quickly sift through the books for the coloured dots.

In a nutshell:

1. Teach pupils the school's **marking policy** and basic **proofreading symbols**, as this will reduce your marking workload considerably. Pupils will quickly understand that you have a clearly thought-out marking system and act on it.

2. Be as **succinct** and **positive** as possible in your comments.

3. Use **stamps** and **stickers** for motivational purposes and use **sharply focused learning objectives** and **success criteria** to precisely mark work against.

Smarter Marking

Notes

Chapter 7
Have Yourself a Terrific Transition Day!

When you start your new role, it is highly likely that you will be visiting your new class on Transition Day; this is where you need to set out your stall, start as you mean to go on and be the best kind of classroom teacher you would want to see in the world.

In my opinion, many teachers make the mistake of doing soft, light and fluffy lessons or solely 'fun' lessons on Transition Day, but this is probably the worst thing you can do, as it will give pupils the impression that your lessons will always be high-octane entertainment. I am not suggesting that your Transition Day is Victorian in nature and that you don't do some ice-breaking activities but the **whole day should not proceed in this fashion**. You need to give your students a taste of your **teaching style**, **routines and classroom expectations**; otherwise, when September whips round and they enter your classroom and your style is completely different to that seen on Transition Day, then they'll potentially see you as a Jekyll and Hyde character and won't trust you. Nothing comes as a surprise to your students once you have effective classroom routines embedded.

After having taught for decades, my teaching instincts are so deeply etched that some of what I do as a teacher in the classroom is second nature now but, hopefully, I have given you a thorough account of a Transition Day experience in this chapter. I wanted to provide you with the component parts of a Transition Day in as much detail as possible, to support planning for your own

Transition Day. Below is a step-by-guide of what I generally do for Year 5 Transition Days.

Preparation: The Day Before 15:45–16:15

On the afternoon prior to Transition Day, after the tables have been cleaned, I write the names of my new class in whiteboard pen on the pupils' desks, as this is quicker than making named cards. My desks are in rows. I know the height of COVID-19 has passed but I still stick with rows as behaviour is better when children are facing the front. Also, it is lovely to have all faces facing forward rather than just pupils' profiles. To help me write the names quickly on desks, I have the seating plan, which I prepared in advance, displayed on my interactive whiteboard (IWB) in PowerPoint. If you're lucky, you would have already had a discussion with the current teacher about seating arrangements during handover sessions. I have used table cards with pupils' names in the past, but the whiteboard pen is simpler and saves on card, cutting and folding or having to purchase table cards. If your tables are not laminated or smooth, you will have to use table cards because ink removal can be more difficult on porous and granular surfaces.

If you are new to the school and have not had any handover about the personalities of your class-to-be and do not yet have access to your new classroom, then a better option would be to use table cards/mats/tags. If this is not possible because you have not been provided with a register for your new class, give each child an address label upon entry for them to write their name on, and instruct them to sit where they would like, the proviso being that they place themselves next to someone with whom they work well. I did this once and it was fascinating to see where pupils chose to sit. During a quiet moment, I took a note of where everyone decided to sit. On this occasion, this free rein approach made it easier for me to formulate a seating plan because, for the most part, pupils were sensible and did sit next to people with whom they got along. From the outset, it also gave me insight into the friendship groups of the class.

Again, if you're fortunate, your class will come with equipment from their current classroom, but I always buy packs of cheap pencils just in case. I also ensure that there is an ample supply of plain and lined paper. I try to avoid gluing and the use of worksheets on Transition Day, to focus purely on the learning. If I do use task or reference sheets, I ensure that this is copied at the beginning of the week because if you leave Transition Day resourcing to the last minute, you will almost certainly end up spending most of your time standing in line for the photocopier.

I place a **pencil**, **green colouring pencil**, **ruler** and some **squared paper** for each pupil on their tables, as the morning task will be a maths task.

As per usual, I ensure that I have a visual timetable or poster showing pupils the structure of the morning or day, as this is particularly important for some neurodivergent pupils. What works for neurodivergent pupils is good practice and generally works for all.

Arrival

Be early! I'm an early bird and tend to arrive at school at 07:30 or earlier on most days. Check that your IWB and slideshows work. At 08:45, when Transition Day officially begins, my day starts outside in the corridor by my classroom. I have lost count of the number of times I have had pupils just enter their soon-to-be classroom without permission; therefore, manners are something I drill into them from the beginning. You want to have controlled entry into your classroom. You are the captain of your classroom, and your pupils need to understand that. I line up my new class and check their uniforms before entry. You need to sweat the small stuff because if you don't, standards and behaviour slip quickly. I then gently but emphatically explain to children that they must never enter a classroom without an adult for reasons of good manners as well as health and safety.

Tip: If you wish, you could have some classical music playing gently in the background in the mornings to create a calm start.

I dial up my personality and warmly welcome the class, telling them to enter the class in silence for the purposes of calm and concentration. I try to use positive language and phrasing all the time, as I find this more effective than being a drill sergeant. For example, rather than barking, "Wipe your feet, please!" I turn the language around and thank pupils for wiping their feet. This is a gentle, pre-emptive, exasperation-free method which keeps the atmosphere warm and friendly. I tell them that their names are on the tables and that the seating plan is also on the screen, helping them to their seats if they can't work out where to go. I avoid saying phrases, such as 'Welcome boys and girls!' and avoid games and competitions which separate teams according to gender, as this could be uncomfortable for certain pupils.

Once the class members are all inside, I take the register and explicitly tell them how I wish them to respond; for example, for some teachers, it is acceptable for pupils to answer with a: "Yes, miss/sir" but I insist on being called by my title and surname, as I want my class to understand that everyone is an individual. If you succinctly give reasons for your expectations, children are generally accepting.

I then ask a member of the class nearest to the fire drill register to take the fire drill register whilst I am taking the school register. This immediately shows the class that I expect them to take responsibility for some of the classroom administration.

After the register, I teach them the following chant to set the tone for learning. I have it displayed on the IWB on a PowerPoint. It is a well-known chant that I learned when I went on a World War 2 educational trip. Here it is:

> **Good, better, best. Never let it rest. 'Til your good is better and your better is best.**

I explain to the class that they will do a Morning Maths task every morning and that they will all have an individual reading book, which they can read in silence after they have finished their

Have Yourself a Terrific Transition Day!

Morning Maths task when they join me in September. Reading is incredibly important and having an arrival task as well as embedded reading routines set the tone.

Later in the year, I also add 'Next steps' to the morning task; in other words, once they have finished their morning maths task, they examine their marked work in maths, English and Guided Reading and act on teacher feedback provided. This is, in effect, what is sometimes referred to as Dedicated Improvement Reflection Time (**DIRT**).

At the beginning of my career, I used to devise my own calculations or borrow content from my maths textbooks, which took a great deal of time for something that only took pupils five or ten minutes to do. However, I now save time by using online resources, such as *Maths Shed*, which currently provides *Quick Maths* PowerPoints per term, with answers attached. The slides were worth the money because they linked to the National Curriculum and freed me up to carry out lesson planning.

Firstly, I tell the children to draw a margin measuring two squares in width. I instruct them to write their first name and second name at the top left of the paper and leave a square's space. Then they must write the title 'Morning Maths' and underline with a ruler and pencil as shown here:

Morning Maths
1. 622 + 719 = _____
2. 500 - ____ = 120
3. 144 divided by 12 = _____
4. _____ = 8,473 – 1,000
5. ½ + ¼ = _____

I then set my timer to eight minutes and ask them to complete the five abstract calculations independently within the time prescribed on the squared paper provided, using a pencil and writing the number for each calculation in the margin. I circulate the classroom, supporting and carrying out live marking as I go, as well as making a mental note of the children's mathematical fluency. From this short, simple exercise, I gain a good idea of how well they listen to and follow instructions, manipulate a ruler (hand-eye co-ordination), written presentation and their maths knowledge. You can insert timers into PowerPoints but sometimes they take up too much space on slides, so I prefer to use my basic timer as detailed in Chapter 1.

On the main whiteboard, for those who breezed through the questions, I have an open-ended maths task, such as: *How many calculations can you think of that equal 40? Use a range of mathematical operations.*

Once the timer goes off, I elicit pupils' responses and share the answers on the IWB one at a time, asking them for the most efficient methods and which calculations they were able to do mentally. Pupils neatly self-assess with their editing pens (if they have one) or a green colouring pencil provided. This is a great opportunity to listen to pupils, celebrate their successes and encourage those who may not have correctly answered the questions. I smile when pupils provide wrong and correct answers and thank them for their contributions, as no-one likes to be taken for granted. I inform the children that alongside my verbal and written feedback they, too, will be taking responsibility for monitoring and self-marking their own work, particularly in maths. Encouraging your class to be active participants in their learning and marking of work will **significantly reduce your workload**. I always check that my pupils have marked their maths correctly and that they have used efficient methods, etc., but it does cut my marking time considerably when they can mark abstract maths accurately from a mark scheme provided. It is vital that as a teacher you succinctly narrate the key points you wish to highlight as you go along to establish routines but try not to over-instruct; be economical with your language; otherwise, your pupils may feel bombarded by too much information.

Housekeeping

Once this task has been completed, I tell them to place their pencils on the table like cutlery and to sit up and fold their arms as they are going to listen to key classroom expectations. Setting your stall early by having a clear behaviour system anchors you and your students, which allows them to quickly feel at ease in the classroom. This is where I introduce Doug Lemov's **SLANT,** which promotes active listening skills and basic classroom etiquette:

Sitting up straight
Listening
Asking and answering questions
Never interrupting others
Tracking the **adults** and **children** who are speaking to the whole class.

You could elicit from children what they feel they need to do to learn successfully and be happy and safe in the classroom, but this usually becomes a long-winded exercise, and I would always advocate economy of language as pupils switch off when teachers drone on and on. **SLANT** is memorable, explicitly clear and does not burden the children in terms of cognitive load because it is so simple to remember. If you're in a value-based school, you could ask pupils how **SLANT** ties in with the school values.

This is also the time that I teach pupils my hand signals for the purpose of instructions and the use of my concierge bell. I use a concierge bell to obtain my children's attention in a calm manner. It also means that I am not having to over-use my voice.

During the height of COVID, I shared the following slide on **hygiene,** and I still insist on good hygiene because COVID has not vanished into the ether and there are many bugs and viruses out there.

- Thank you for keeping up the great handwashing, sanitising hands and the binning of dirty tissues!
- Don't touch your face!
- Use of toilets – one at a time, at set times of the day to prevent wandering.
- Keep your workspace **tidy** and **clear of clutter**, too, as this makes for a more pleasant, clean and comfortable work environment.

I go through my routines and expectations, including lining up. I worked in a school where all pupils had to walk around the school when filing up for assembly, break time and lunch time with their hands behind their backs. Since it was a part of the whole school culture, conduct around the school was exemplary. Even if you're in a school that does not espouse this, it is still worth teaching because it instantly means 'kind hands and kind feet' and prevents poor behaviour during lining up.

I spend a bit of time on the **Reporting V Tattling** because in the past I taught a Year 4 class who were sometimes incredibly gleeful when it came to their classmates getting into trouble, and I had to continually tell them the difference between reporting and tattling throughout the year. Clearly explaining the difference to your pupils at the beginning of the academic year greatly minimises potential tattling issues.

A culture of kindness is inculcated in my pupils from the moment they arrive, and I teach them to notice the feelings of others, to celebrate each other's successes, to listen and self-regulate – the idea being that we strive to treat everyone in school as a friend and that we make a positive impact on our environment. You need to model the behaviour you want to see. This allows pupils to feel comfortable in the class and not fear making mistakes. The well-known **T.H.I.N.K.** acronym sums this up beautifully (please see Chapter 4 for wording). To finish off, we chant this a couple of times to end on a positive note.

Sadly, pupils are becoming less self-sufficient; for example, nowadays it is not uncommon for a Key Stage 2-aged child to ask a staff member to tie their shoelaces, etc., which is why it is also important to teach **pupils soft skills and manners** wherever possible. With each passing year, I find myself carrying out more and more parental duties with pupils; for example, I have demonstrated how to hold a knife and fork in the school dining room; how to peel a banana; and modelled to Year 4 children how to put on a school tie.

Increasingly, lower down in the school, teachers are faced with a growing number of pupils (without additional needs) who are attending school in nappies because they have not yet been toilet trained! Pupils should be taught basic etiquette and skills by their parents; however, some parents either do not want to, or cannot, support or engage with their children in this way, and it then falls on teachers to make up this shortfall.

Structure of the Day

Lesson 1: Mathematics 09:15–10:25

On Transition Day, I teach core subjects as I want to see with my own eyes what pupils know. It is sometimes tempting to do other teaching bits and bobs when pupils are working quietly and sensibly but it is important to be present with the children, so don't do other activities. I tell them that I am looking for a **tremendous transition as seamless transitions maximise learning time.** Again, I am succinctly narrating and reminding the class of classroom expectations: teachers are conductors conducting everyone in the class orchestra together. Teaching core subjects on Transition Day may be viewed as unusual by some, as many teachers prefer to do 'Wow Day' type sessions, such as baking or arts and craft. There is nothing wrong with carrying out these sessions as they are a fun and enjoyable way of breaking the ice with your new class; however, I prefer to provide pupils with a taster of what to generally expect in the forthcoming academic year.

In my opinion, Transition Day is not the time for experimentation or to throw caution to the wind, as such activities can go drastically wrong. Transition Day is a day for establishing your credibility and authority as a teacher, getting to know your pupils, introducing routines and expectations and establishing your new pupils' starting points. Having routines leads to calm, comfortable, safe, and productive relationships with automaticity, which saves time. Later in the year, when you have learned more about your class, you can experiment and do more practical tasks, such as cooking, sewing, etc., as then you will know their levels of ability and with whom they work well.

I always do a place value lesson for KS2 on Transition Day and keep things **simple**. Understanding place value is fundamental and this lesson serves as great way of determining pupils' prior knowledge. If there are significant gaps in place value, then this is an area that will be revisited in depth the following September.

Here is an outline of my Transition Day maths lesson.

1. I instruct the pupils to leave one square's space and rule off their previous piece of work, which was Morning Maths, and copy the date and learning objective.

<u>L.O.: To partition numbers in different ways.</u>

2. As a warmup, I share a maths joke to relax the class, for example "Why is 6 scared of seven? Because seven eight nine". With the power of *Google*, you can quickly find a range of pupil-friendly maths jokes to magpie. Also, telling them a joke gives me some insight into their understanding of humour, etc., and then I instruct the class to do a verbal starter:

> How else can we partition the number 86?

3. I circulate because I am always keen to listen to pupils speak and uncover their verbal skills as well as their current **mathematical vocabulary**.

4. Then it's whole-class feedback time. I elicit from the class what place value is about before providing them with a dictionary definition. If a teaching assistant is present, I will ensure that they have a copy of an **overview** of the day and **involve** them in class discussions. I've been blessed to have worked with some incredible TAs and have learnt so much from them, as many have worked in education for several years across different Key Stages and have a great deal of knowledge. In my opinion, skilled teaching assistants truly are the backbone of some schools, and I know that I would not have survived working in some schools without them.

5. I then put place value in real-life context with each numbered point fading in one at a time so as not to split their attention.

6. Then I follow this up with some Guided Practice on mini whiteboards, for example:

This is a **four-digit** number. How do you think we would say this number? **2,367**

What is the three worth? **2,367 and so on.**

---

7. Using this same number, I ask the class the value of X, etc. Pupils record their answers on their whiteboards, keeping a tally of what they have got right. I use graded questions and choral work to build the confidence of the class. If there are some pupils who have not yet voluntarily made verbal contributions, I will ask them questions, as it is important that everyone contributes verbally to lessons. I monitor the class carefully to involve everyone. You may wish to use the lollipop sticks (as explained in Chapter 1) to support questioning.

8. I elicit from the children some other numbers, starting off with 4-digit numbers, and then progressing onto 5-digit and 6-digit numbers, writing them on a flipchart. I ask volunteers to throw a die to make this more randomised. For example, if a pupil throws a die four times and the first throw is 1; the second 3; the third throw 4; and the fourth throw 2, then the number written on the flipchart would be 1,342. I ask the whole class to read the number to practise reading numbers and then instruct them to partition and record their answers on mini whiteboards. This is another opportunity for the consolidation of place value headings, for example:

> The number 3,456 partitioned is 3000 + 400 + 50 + 6

Using the mini whiteboards gives you, as the teacher, instant feedback and you can instantly nip any misconceptions in the bud, quickly moving on if pupils are confident and secure.

9. I ask the children to tell me how they are feeling about their learning based on the traffic light system. I tell all pupils to put their heads down on their desks (for privacy and sensitivity reasons) and to place a thumb up if they feel they understand today's learning and could teach someone what they learned; a thumb on its side if they are almost there; thumb down if they need to be re-taught.

10. To build up confidence, I play a game of noughts and crosses! The game is differentiated in three ways with positive level labels: super, mega and ultra. Super is colour-coded green (least fluent); mega is colour-coded pink (medium fluency); and ultra is colour-coded purple (high fluency). I avoid using levelled categories, such as: 'silver, gold, bronze' and 'red, yellow, green' and the *Nando* 'chilli' approach, such as 'spicy, medium hot, super-hot' because it is immediately obvious what the levels mean and when 'challenge by choice' is offered, some children will always go for the easiest option, even when they are capable of the more advanced tasks. I want pupils to be motivated to carefully read and

select the calculations they can access, rather than going straight for the option that they can easily identify at first glance as novice, intermediate and advanced. Initially, I give pupils three minutes to answer as many questions as they can on their squared paper, and then we play a whole-class game of noughts and crosses. I roughly divide the class into two teams A and B, and we begin. It always goes down well, and it is another opportunity to reinforce knowledge.

L.O.: To partition numbers in different ways.		
Quick game of noughts and crosses! Key: Super Green Mega Pink Ultra Purple	Consolidation!	
$186 = 100 + 80 + ?$	Take 300 from 5,924	Add 100 to 374
What is the value of the digit underlined? 54<u>6</u>	$732 = 700 + ? + 2$	Complete 3,472 = ? + 72
Two million, five hundred and three thousand, two hundred and fourteen	Partition this number: 3,597	What is the value of the digit underlined? 3,1<u>8</u>9

Picture 33: Noughts and Crosses

11. Finally, pupils complete a challenge by choice, differentiated **independent task**. I photocopy fifteen copies of this slide, so that there is one between two, just in case pupils find it difficult to read from the IWB. I usually give pupils 20–25 minutes for an independent task and I circulate with a marking pen so I can do live marking. I also carry a whiteboard pen so that I can write examples on pupils' whiteboards to help them further with their understanding.

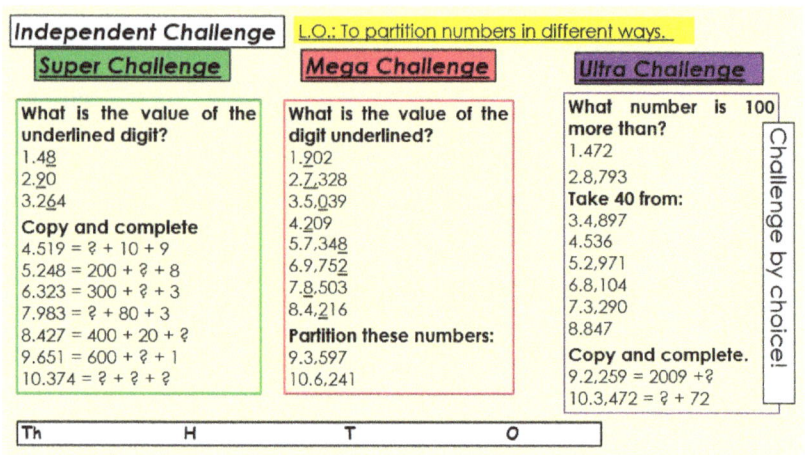

Picture 34: Independent Task

This task is based on material adapted from **Target Your Maths** textbooks, Years 4 & 5, by Stephen Pearce. **Target Your Maths** is one of my maths lesson planning staples and I thoroughly recommend that you buy a relevant year copy for yourself. If pupils finish early, I provide SATs-style questions that I copied from *Testbase,* which is a paid online resource full of SATs questions and past papers.

Some schools use bought-in maths schemes which may not differentiate in the three-strand way; therefore, you will need to take this into account when planning for the year ahead.

12. On the following slide, I have a copy of the mark scheme which I label **'Tick and fix!'** Pupils are then instructed to self-mark with an editing pen or green-coloured pencil.

13. To finish off the lesson, we do a plenary activity:

> Show the value of 6 in each of these numbers.
>
> **6**,462
>
> 34**6**
>
> **6**62
>
> 7,62**3**
>
> Explain how you know.

Then I ask pupils to leave their written work in a neat pile on their tables, and then I nominate one person from each table to place the work from their table underneath my IWB. At lunchtime, I will look at the work produced, making quick notes in my A5 diary about the least fluent mathematicians and pupils who excelled; for example, this year, I taught a pupil who was a very able mathematician, and I knew from the Transition Day that I would need to have additional resources in place to meet his needs. I then place the work in a plastic wallet with an address label on the front: '**Maths Transition Day + date**' and keep it on the top shelf. This can be used as evidence of progression later in the following academic cycle.

Before Break 10:25–10:30

Dismiss table by table to have a staggered dismissal. Pupils still in the classroom can clear their stationery whilst others are collecting their coats from the corridor. I use the same dismissal approach at home time, too. Then instruct them to arrange themselves in register order without talking. They do not leave until they are silent; if that means they lose some of their break, then so be it. I wait for silence and stillness from my pupils rather than nag at them. I will say, "When you're ready," as a gentle reminder. Whilst they are lining up, I tell them that I expect to see stillness and silence as well as marvellous manners and great gaps. Using alliteration in your teaching makes content memorable and catchy; therefore, I use it as much as possible. I picked up this catchy technique from a creative headteacher in a school where I once worked. It is also worth noting that using stories and songs are also great for helping children to learn and remember information. My instructional language is repetitive as I use the same stock phrases (some of my pupils are so well versed in my teacher instructions that they can reel off my spiel!)

Next, I tell the class that when I collect them from the playground, I want them in register order as this is useful during fire drills. When collecting them, check to see if they have lined up in register order by bringing the fire drill list with you.

Break 10:30–10:45

I make a toilet visit straightaway. Fifteen minutes fly, so every second counts. Afterwards, I have a little snack and drink from my thermos flask.

Breaktime Collection: 10:45

At 10:44, I head down to the playground to collect my class with my fire drill list in tow. I check that they have lined up in register order and make them repeat the process with minimal fuss, if they haven't. This is something that I continue throughout the year as it usually (not always) minimises chatting, as the children are less likely to be next to their friends and they quickly learn how to line up alphabetically with ease when a real fire drill happens. If pupils take longer than expected, remember to be **calm, kind** and **relentless**.

Lesson 2: English 10:45–12:00

I try to stick to **one** learning objective for English Transition Day lessons. This allows the pupils to study one English component in-depth and allows me to gauge how successful they have been in their prior learning. Due to Transition Day being a one-off event, I prefer to deliver straightforward consolidation lessons rather than entirely new learning, as it eases the children in and does not faze them as much. You must remember that anxiety will be high amongst some pupils, and you want to ensure that your pupils feel **comfortable** and **accomplished**. One of the reasons for Transition

Day is to put pupils at ease in preparation for the upcoming new term in September. Here is the outline:

1. Whenever the opportunity arises, I like to see what children observe and begin with a discussion SPaG starter strongly linked to the lesson. On my slide, I include a short piece of text I found in a book years ago, whose name escapes me, about a dragon. The text contains no adjectives. The title of the starter is 'What's Missing?'. I highlight all the nouns in blue and verbs in green to introduce my system of colour coding for SPaG. I read the text aloud to the class. Apologies but for reasons of copyright, I am unable to reproduce the text I use here; however, below is what I produced to give you a quick idea to show you what I mean:

> Slowly, the monster unveiled its wings and opened its mouth to reveal rows of teeth. It curled its claws into a ball. Menacingly, the creature widened its eyes and peered into its prey's soul.

2. Once it has been established that the text contains no adjectives, I move onto the aim of the lesson by sharing the L.O. and differentiated S.C.:

L.O.: To use up-levelled vocabulary to describe a dragon.

Success Criteria:

- To know what an **adjective** is.
- To recognise the **importance of adjectives** in narratives.
- To use **high-quality adjectives** in story writing.

3. I explain to the children that they are going to learn about adjectives. They will be spotting adjectives in what they read and looking at how adding interesting adjectives improves writing. During the entire lesson, I speak in full sentences, using aspirational language and high-level vocabulary. Nowadays, it has become common for some people to use the word 'like' repeatedly as a filler. If this is something you

do in your daily speech, I urge you to try to avoid using 'like' as a filler whilst you are teaching, as 'like' should principally be used as a verb.

4. Next, I ask the children what an adjective is before revealing a dictionary definition with examples on my PowerPoint.

5. I then elicit from the class the purpose of adjectives.

6. Using the text from the starter (I am big on recycling material as it makes learning stickier), I have the text on a slide but, this time, with spaces for adjectives to go (please see below). I ask pupils to think of adjectives associated with dragons. I explain that we could pair adjectives to add depth to writing and include similes. I share a high-quality image of a fierce dragon with the children (not cartoonish) to inspire them.

> Slowly, the_____ monster unveiled its _____ wings and opened its _____mouth to reveal rows of _____teeth. It curled its _____claws into a _____ ball. Menacingly, the creature widened its _____ eyes and peered into its prey's soul.

7. I ask a pupil to be a Magpie Assistant, which means a volunteer pupil records the vocabulary given by their classmates on a flipchart. By recording pupils' vocabulary on flipchart paper, a word bank is available for all to use during the lesson. I am looking for examples of figurative language from fluent learners and expecting synonyms for the word 'dragon' (examples: beast, creature, monster, fire-breather) as well as adjectives, such as frightening, ferocious, wild, etc.

8. On the following slide, I provide a WAGOLL (What a Good One Looks Like) with high-level vocabulary choices of my own, which we discuss. In some instances, the pupils come

up with other excellent ideas to improve my work which, again, allows pupils to be exposed to language-rich text.

9. I then explain that descriptive writing can be let down by using boring language, such as *big, small, nice, scary* (please see section 'Banned Words' in Chapter 4 for more details).

10. **Independent Task:** On lined paper, pupils write a description of a cute or frightening dragon with a variety of adjectives. I will tell pupils that if they are describing a cute dragon, 'menacing' and 'ferocious' are not words that we would use. Again, I am reiterating how an image in one's mind can be transformed by adjectives, and vocabulary needs to be specific to context. I ensure that I have a writing frame for less fluent writers and differentiate the task in three ways as shown below:

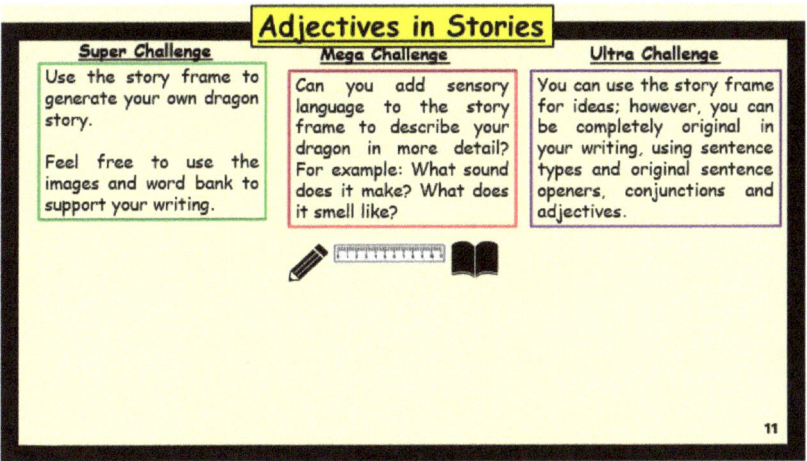

Picture 35: Independent Challenge

The writing frame I use is a scaffold called 'Adjectives in Stories' from www.Teacher-of-Primary.co.uk which is inserted into my PowerPoint. The scaffold is a short description about a dragon, which has gaps where adjectives could go.

11. For the most fluent writers, I will provide a word list by extracting key language from *Descriptosaurus Supporting Creative Writing for ages 8 – 14* by Alison Wilcox and reiterate that they use exciting **verbs**, **adverbs** and **similes.**

12. During the lesson, I will do live marking and talk with pupils about their ideas and writing. I usually set a timer for the main task with my 'terrific timer' to ensure that we manage our time well.

13. As an **extension**, I provide another dragon description for pupils to up-level.

14. Next, pupils proofread their work and read their work aloud to a classmate, explaining why they have chosen certain adjectives and how they could improve their writing.

15. Nearing the end of the lesson, I ask for volunteers to share their work under the visualiser as this gives pupils a further opportunity to learn from others. This is 'Celebration of Success'.

I ask the children how they are feeling about their learning based on the traffic light system and if they can remember the S.C. If no-one attempted the extension, we do this together, too, if there is time available. Finally, I collect their written work as detailed in the maths lesson earlier.

Reading Aloud to the Class 12:00

'Cosy Reading', 'Daily Reading' or 'Shared Reading', whatever you choose to call this part of the day is fine by me, as long as you are reading aloud to your class effectively. Reading is incredibly important for **accessing the curriculum, creativity, independence** and **vocabulary building** and should be actively encouraged in pupils. One of the simplest ways in which pupils' reading can be improved is by their teacher reading to them: you are best placed to model fluent and expressive reading. Reading needs to be brought to life through employing different voices, accents and giving your all to the performance. Your passion and enthusiasm when reading aloud will rub off on your pupils. In any case, teachers need to ignite the spirit of the dramatic performer within them to inspire their students. Sadly, for some children, you may be the only adult that reads to them.

If you read in a monotone manner, this is unlikely to spark interest amongst your pupils. It is important for your class to see reading in action by seeing how the written word can be translated to the spoken word. I recommend always having a **classroom reader** that you share with the class on a daily basis. Try to select a book that you can complete each term, as pupils feel cheated when they don't get to finish a book in its entirety. For example, I comfortably read all of Michael Morpurgo's *Kensuke's Kingdom* in the first term and the class thoroughly enjoyed it. Some parts of both texts were so moving that some of us were moved to tears (me included). That's the power of great literature; it has the power to touch us emotionally, which is part of the human experience. Make certain that you read the book in full beforehand, so you are fully familiar with it, know the voices you wish to assign to characters, and to check that all of the text is suitable, etc.

If possible, have enough copies of the class reader available so that pupils can follow along as you read. If not, you could try looking to see if any free PDF copies are online. During COVID, some books were scanned by schools and uploaded for free online; therefore, I found an electronic PDF copy of *Kensuke's Kingdom*, which I displayed online whilst reading to the class.

After I finish reading to my class, I reiterate that we will be reading on a daily basis and I promote my **class library** at this moment, telling them that they can pick a book and read for pleasure. At this point, they are settled and ready for dismissal. I follow the same drill as outlined in the maths lesson but, this time, the children are instructed to wash their hands.

Whilst they are performing hand washing or sanitiser application, I teach the class the T.H.I.N.K. acronym and we chant a couple of times. I do this to encourage children to think about their behaviour outside of the classroom. I'm not saying it's a magic wand but in the event of lunchtime incidents, you can use T.H.I.N.K. as a script to question pupils about what happened and their reactions; for example, if a child did react badly, you could ask them: 'Was that kind?' etc. I also remind pupils to go the toilet before the end of lunch so as not to disturb our afternoon lessons.

Lunchtime: 12:15-13:15

I have a look at the English work and do the same as before for the maths lesson: I simply look through the work completed to form an overall picture of the class and make some notes in my diary; this usually takes 15-20 minutes. Due to my palpable COVID fears (which have never left me), I clean my teacher desk with a cleaning wipe; wash my hands; and eat my packed lunch. Whilst I am in the classroom, some students enter the classroom to collect their water bottles, and this is when I teach them to knock and wait before entering. Once I have finished my lunch, I pop outside for a bit of fresh air at the front of the school building for five minutes. After this brief respite, I visit the toilet and get ready to collect the children from the playground, checking that the pupils have lined up in alphabetical order quietly, as before during break.

Afternoon Registration: 13:15-13: 25

During afternoon registration, I share a screenshot which informs what I expect after lunch. Once the children are in their seats, I tell them that I know that they do not yet have their reading books; therefore, they will need to sit in silence whilst I take the register.

Thankfully, there are no lunchtime issues to sort out. One of my bug bears is unresolved issues at lunchtime. I do reiterate to pupils that they should seek help at lunchtime from the midday supervisors and senior teachers on duty, but it tends to go in one ear and out the other.

After the register, I put *Newsround* on as this is a great settler and give pupils a chance to discuss current affairs.

I will always allow a child to go to the toilet, but some pupils ask to go to the toilet even though they have just had lunch! This is where I teach them the French for 'May I go to the toilet, please?' The majority of my pupils will remember to go to the toilet at lunch time because they do not want to go to the trouble of having to ask in French.

Lesson 3: History & Art 13:30–15:00

For the first part of the afternoon, I teach a lesson that is connected to a history topic, such as the Vikings. I combine history and art because I get to see how well pupils can retain knowledge and how good their art is. Art is another great way of assessing pupils; for example, how do they manipulate their pencil? Is there attention to detail or is the work well below age-related expectations? Are the pupils colouring in within lines?

1. I present the learning objective and then the title page of the lesson and discuss the word 'Viking' because it is likely that not all children will know about them.

> **L.O.: To design a Viking shield using historical knowledge.**

2. The next slide contains a Talk Pairs starter with the question: Why do you think Vikings used shields?
3. I will then tell the pupils that later in the year, they will be studying the book *Beowulf* by Michael Morpugo, which features tales of battle, heroism, monsters and good against evil. At this point, I share some of the less frightening book covers of *Beowulf*. I tell them about the importance of the original *Beowulf* in terms of English literature and that it is an epic poem written in Old English. Again, I share some images from online. I will then introduce the fact that some of the characters were armed with weapons, such as wooden shields and this allows me to segue into Viking shields.
4. I will give a brief description of Viking shields, namely: circular, wooden, large (approximately a metre across), with an iron boss at the centre to protect the hand.

5. Discussion Point: I will ask pupils why archaeologists have not found much evidence of complete shields except for the central boss and some metal fittings. Hopefully, pupils will say something along the lines that wooden shields would have decayed with the passage of time. This often leads to questions from the children, such as: How heavy were the shields? Did the warriors have to be strong? Did women fight? It is worth pointing out to the class that some women fought in battle and were called Shield Maidens.
6. I share some examples of shields that I found online. Sorry I cannot reproduce them here for reasons of copyright.
7. Discussion Point: Why were the shields colourful? Accept possible answers, such as: to frighten the enemy; to create a sense of united spirit amongst the warriors.
8. I also share how shields were used, in a short video showing a fighting tactic called 'Shield Wall' https://www.youtube.com/watch?v=D-NDVhoGjO0 (fast forward to Chapter Shield Wall).
9. I hand out a blank shield template as shown and tell the class that these shields will be going on display for September; this encourages pupils to work to the best of their ability. The template looks like this:
10. I ask volunteers to hand out packs of colouring pencils for each table.
11. Time passes and before you know it, it's dismissal for home time. Packing away is as performed previously, except this time they gather their belongings from their lockers and then return to the classroom. I explain the packing away procedure to them to avoid time wastage and display it on a PowerPoint.

- Ensure your name is on your work.
- Each table is to pass their colouring pencils and worksheets towards the inner aisle, making certain that

the sheets are the right way up and arranged in a neat pile.
- The table that is tidy with pupils waiting beautifully will be the first to collect their belongings from lockers.

I set the timer for packing away to three minutes.

So, that's one of my Transition Days in a nutshell. Nothing comes as a shock to your students once you have effective classroom routines embedded, and having rituals is comforting and allows for a more relaxed atmosphere.

Ending Transition Day

Before the end of the Transition Day, I like to do some 'Getting to Know You' games, such as 'Truth or Fib' and 'Guess Who'. You can find many examples of simple games online that **require little or no resourcing.**

In the past, I used to provide a letter template for pupils to write their hobbies, interests, hopes for the future, but found that many pupils had previously done this before as part of Transition Days. Instead, you may wish to do this type of activity with your current class; for example, a teacher I know used this as part of one of her letter writing English lessons. During our handover session, she gave me copies of the letters the class had written to me. Due to the fact that the letters were written in the context of an English unit on letter writing rather than a one-off lesson, the letters were delightful, well written and helpful because pupils told me things they thought I should know about them.

Morning-only Transition

In instances where I am with my class for only a morning, I structure the day as follows:

Seating Plan	(5–10 mins)
Morning Maths	Same as previously outlined (5–10 mins)
Registration	(5 mins)
Expectations	(10 mins)

Maths	(1 hr)
Assembly	Delivered by SLT (20–30 mins)
Break	(15 mins)
English	Proofreading (1 hr)
'Getting to Know You' Shield templates	(1hr 15 mins)

English

Due to time constraints for a morning-only Transition session, I do a different lesson for English, which focuses on proofreading. I have received positive feedback from pupils regarding this lesson. We focus solely on spelling, punctuation and grammatical areas rather than editing sentences; this is how the lesson goes:

1. Firstly, I share an example of writing from a previous pupil, which clearly demonstrates expectations for presentation in Year 5. It contains pupils' editing in purple as well as the marking (proofreading) codes that they will learn about in the following lesson.

2. The next slide shows the L.O. and the differentiated S.C.:

L.O.: To practise proofreading skills.
S.C.:
- I can take part in **discussions** regarding proofreading.
- I can use **proofreading symbols**.
- I can **proofread a piece of real-life text**.

---

3. Each slide has the L.O. at the top. The third slide provides the question 'What is proofreading?' with a corresponding definition in animated form with bullet points (maximum five bullet points).

4. Slide 4 shows a piece of text that looks like gobbledygook yet we, as humans, are able to read it. The reason for this slide is to show pupils that we read words as a whole rather than reading every letter. Unfortunately, I cannot display the text here for reasons of copyright.

5. I show a video about proofreading; it's a video from the BBC. Here it is: https://www.bbc.co.uk/bitesize/articles/zpyhtyc#zhgsrmn.

6. Pupils need to have their whiteboards ready for the next 11 images. The images are **real-life** examples featuring a range of spelling and grammatical errors. I tell the children that I am looking for hawk-eyed spotters. I like to link learning to real-life contexts as this is another way of helping pupils to remember new content. Again, unfortunately, I cannot share these due to copyright but if you enter search parameters online for notices/adverts with errors, etc., you can generate examples.

7. I discuss proofreading strategies, such as reading from the bottom up, slowing down, reading in sections, reading aloud, working for a partner, spelling errors (homophones), avoiding text speak and then share some proofreading symbols. These proofreading symbols are based on a typical school's marking policy. Most schools have adopted similar codes to the ones I have listed here but if the codes below do not match with your school's policy, then adapt accordingly:

CL = capital letters

_ = lower case letter

P = punctuation

Sp = spellings

^ = missing information

g = grammar

~?~ = Sentence sense

// = new paragraph

= space

/ = eliminate

↑ = up-level

8. I guide the class on how to proofread a piece of text which I have displayed on the PowerPoint. The text is littered with mistakes – all the proofreading symbols will be needed to identify the errors.

9. Once pupils have seen how proofreading symbols are used to identify mistakes, they are given a **differentiated** independent task. One is a fictional menu with seven mistakes to find (lower level of challenge) and the other is a polite letter from a parent addressed to a teacher, asking for her daughter's detention to be put off until another day (higher level of challenge). They write directly on the task sheet.

Although I enjoy composing my own tasks and models, it is important to recognise that you don't have to reinvent the wheel, as you can use suitable educational resources in books or online. The only downside right now is that I cannot provide a copy of them here for reasons of copyright – sorry!

10. The penultimate slide is a 'Recipe for Success in Year 5' poem. It is a poem that I found online, which I copied and adapted to include a range of spelling errors for pupils to find and correct. To make it more accessible, I wrote the number of errors per line in brackets. I thought this was a lovely way to end the lesson as it reinforces values, positivity and kindness, and provides another opportunity to practise proofreading.

11. The last slide is a copy of the L.O. and S.C. slide, which serves as a plenary. I elicit from pupils what they have learned by referring to the success criteria.

Getting to Know You

1. Instead of the Viking shield activity, I provide pupils with a shield template that I found on *Kapow Primary*. It is a shield divided into four quadrants. Each quadrant has a heading:

- I enjoy
- My personality
- I am good at
- I am proud of

Underneath the shield is a banner in which pupils can write their name.

2. I share previous pupil examples of shields to show children what I am looking for. Pupils are instructed to write relevant content underneath each heading and then decorate their shields.

3. Pupils neatly write their names in the banner.

4. I then back these shields on black paper to create a whole-class display for the start of the academic year.

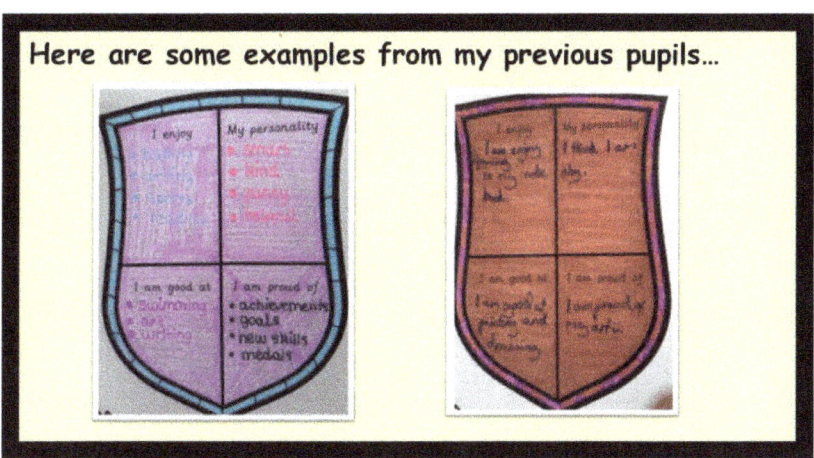

Picture 36: Pupil examples

In a nutshell:

1. **Do not get carried away and do a series of 'soft' activities all day** as you won't truly see how well pupils interact with one another or uncover their academic ability.

2. To enjoy a seamless Transition Day, **keep it as simple and well planned** as possible. If your creative juices aren't flowing, you can find WAGOLL examples in educational books or online - you **don't always have to reinvent the wheel!** As author Anthony J. D'Angelo said, "**Don't reinvent the wheel, just realign it.**" Although I use PowerPoint, it is not death-by-PowerPoint; ensure that there are

opportunities for class-based discussion, mini whiteboard work and flipchart sheets. Also, it is good to have a spread of resources just in case technology fails.

3. **Share your classroom expectations** in a succinct, scripted manner from the outset to pre-empt potential behavioural issues, and ensure that this is narrated during your lessons to drip-feed high standards. If you are **calm, kind** and **relentless at all times**, then this will serve you well.

Have Yourself a Terrific Transition Day!

Notes

Chapter 8
Principles of Lesson Planning

Creating memorable learning experiences for my students holds a special place in my heart. Without successful lesson planning, there cannot be successful learning, which is why I find it difficult to understand teachers who have an aversion to lesson planning. Why become a teacher if you don't like lesson planning? It's an essential component of the job. If you constantly moan about lesson planning, then I would question whether teaching is for you. Here are some points, in three-fold, that I would like to make in respect of this:

1. If you have an aversion to hard work, maybe teaching is not the right career for you.
2. If you're not interested in developing subject knowledge or planning engaging, well-sequenced lessons that address the needs of your students, don't be a teacher.
3. If you want to blindly download ready-made lessons for all your subjects without checking them, tweaking or adapting them, and only deliver good/outstanding lessons when SLT or Ofsted are watching, then you shouldn't be a teacher.

Before I hear the clamour of criticism, given that you have bought this book strongly indicates that you are genuinely interested in the serious business of teaching; however, I think it is worth including these statements because, bizarre as it might seem, there are some teachers out there who have no interest in developing their pedagogical skills, and truly loathe and resist lesson planning. I hope that you will never be exposed to such colleagues or worse, have to work with them. Given what I witnessed in various schools as a supply teacher, I know that poor planning is more widespread than schools care to admit, or worse, the SLT aren't aware of what's occurring in their own school.

By creating lessons with your pupils clearly at the forefront, learning outcomes will be more successful; in fact, some of my pupils have been very complimentary about my lessons, commenting on the distinctiveness of the content and their ability to remember them. I am reminded of a quote by educationalist Ken Robinson that I read once, as I always felt that it summed up my thoughts about teaching: "Teaching is a creative profession, not a delivery system. Great teachers do pass on information, but what great teachers also do is mentor, stimulate, provoke and engage."

I am all for magpieing, streamlining and following good practice (as you have already seen in Chapter 7) and using resources such as ready-made slides and lesson plans as a starting point or source of inspiration, because we should not have to reinvent the wheel all the time; however, a teacher who solely uses ready-made, death-by-PowerPoint presentations and reams of worksheets without any adaptation tells me that their heart is not in the job. Reeling off ready-made resources wholesale rarely works; I've nearly always had to adapt what I find online and make my PowerPoints a bit more bespoke. I did a couple of days of supply in a school where pupils had nearly completed an entire poetry unit using ready-made resources but had not even touched upon personification. I think AI will also lead to teachers copying and pasting on a grand scale. Maybe it is a case of more fool me for not using it, but I don't want to enter another digital ghetto and further numb my brain. That said, I may warm to the idea in the future.

Children deserve excellent learning experiences, not a lesson lottery. If pupils are exposed to beautiful, linguistically rich texts, this will develop their communication skills, and they will see education as an adventure.

Now, I am going to provide you with materials and strategies that hopefully will support you in your teaching. This chapter will cover the following areas:

- **Educational Investments** – My textbooks and resources of choice.
- **Headspace for Planning** – Prioritising the best time for lesson planning.
- **Mechanics of Lesson Planning** – The thought processes and what goes into planning units of work in English is what I have chosen to focus on, as primary English is not as easy to plan as other subjects.

Educational Investments

Teaching from a strong foundation requires good subject knowledge and intellectual preparation. Your lessons need to focus on providing knowledge in a memorable way that consolidates learning and enables pupils to recall knowledge in the here and now, as well as in the future. Understanding how memory works is important when teaching lessons. In the past, I used to spend considerable time making PowerPoints pretty, but now I focus on substance over style and as long as my PowerPoints are tidy and uncluttered, I don't worry so much about fancy graphics, etc.

Call me 'old-school', if you like, but I still love textbooks. Below are the ones that serve me well in my core lesson planning and collectively are my simple resource system.

Literacy-based Textbooks

***Improving Story Writing at Key Stages 1 & 2* by Alan Peat**

This is filled with pupil examples and structured activities which build on narrative skills, particularly the power of structure, different openers, sensory language, characterisation and synonym-building.

***Improving Non-fiction Writing at Key Stages 1 & 2: the Success Approach* by Margaret McNeil & Alan Peat**

This was a book which was recommended to me years ago by a fellow teacher when I first became a primary teacher, and it was instrumental during my early years of primary teaching as it is a step-by-step guide on different genres and the specific language linked to certain genres. There are a range of tasks suggested in plain English as well as a plethora of pupil examples and ready-to-use models. In my opinion, my pupil outcomes are living proof that the methodology outlined in this book works. I did not use all the resources and suggested activities, but I did find them useful as they sparked ideas which enabled me to put my own spin on my lessons, following the approach featured in this book as well as drawing on some of Pie Corbett's Talk for Writing framework.

Help Your Kids with English: A Unique Step-by-step Visual Guide by Carol Vorderman

This book is great for SPaG, with easy-to-follow examples of word class with clear colour coding to aid understanding.

Descriptosaurus Supporting Creative Writing for ages 8 – 14 by Alison Wilcox

No teacher's toolkit would be complete without this wonderful book. I absolutely love it as it is packed with a wide range of language assigned to different settings, characters and creatures. I use it in so many ways, such as when writing my own models, personalised word banks and for SPaG starters.

KS2 Comprehension Success by Rachel Axten-Higgs

This is great for KS2 Guided Reading lessons. It includes a range of different texts across fiction, plays, poetry and non-fiction with answers, too.

Picture Books

Picture books, such as Aaron Becker's *Journey* and David Wiesner's *Flotsam* are beautiful and are also great for promoting writing skills.

Online Resources

Alongside my textbooks, I also dip into some online resources; namely, the **Oak Academy** website, which I accessed for free during the pandemic for spelling lessons, science and some grammar lessons; **CGP Plus** (paid subscription) across all subjects, including homework tasks; **Grammarsaurus** (paid subscription) across all subjects; **Vocabulary Ninja** (paid resources) for SPaG starters; and **Plan Bee** (paid resources) for certain foundation subjects.

Pobble 365 is a website that contains some beautiful artwork, which can be used for descriptive writing. Tell children to approach their writing like a camera operative, with each part of the image being zoomed in on by the camera, focussing on every detail. **Literacy Shed** also contains some great videos that can be accessed for free:

- *Alien Invasion*: I used this video during a science fiction unit I planned.

- *For the Birds*: I used this to promote discussions about bullying during Anti-bullying Week. Pupils learned about diary writing features and then wrote diary entries about bullying, using what they had learned from the video.

- *The Switch*: I created a unit on narrative writing around a short advert featuring Cristiano Ronaldo and a young boy who swap bodies.

Maths Textbooks

***Help Your Kids with Maths: A Unique Step-by-step Visual Guide* by Carol Vorderman**

I enjoyed the English version of this so much that I bought the Maths one, too.

CGP Maths for Key Stage 2

Differentiated maths exercises, including both abstract and word problems.

***Target Your Maths Year 5* by Stephen Pearce**

There are *Target Your Maths* textbooks across different year groups. Inside there are examples at the top of every page and the content is aligned with the current National Curriculum Framework of 2014. The book is replete with abstract maths, open-ended maths as well as a range of word problems to solve. It offers a wide range of material for teachers to use in maths lessons.

How to be Good at Maths Workbook 2 by Carol Vorderman

For my least fluent mathematicians, I refer to How to be *Good at Maths Workbook 2* textbook because it contains worked examples at the top of each page and presents mathematics in a visually clear manner.

Top Tip: Ensure that your maths lessons feature a range of abstract, and real-life (open and closed) word problems.

Examples:

- **Real-life (open)** Look at the holiday brochure. Organise a list of activities for a group of 4 adults and work out the cost. Remember, you have a budget.
- **Real-life (closed)** Connie buys 5 apples. Each apple costs 25p. How much does she pay?
- **Abstract (closed)** $9 \times 3 =$
- **Abstract (open)** Pick a number of your choice inside the shape and multiply it by the numbers surrounding the shape.

Testbase

If your school subscribes to this, I advise that you take advantage of it, since the website is replete with SATs questions. I regularly include SATs questions as part of my maths lessons, which means pupils are exposed on a regular basis to SATs-style questions.

Headspace for Planning

I have always done as much marking as possible at school and left lesson planning at home. In previous schools where I had to stay on-site for PPA, apart from discussion with colleagues about the week ahead and general catch-up, I spent most of it marking.

In my previous year team, we divided labour by assigning certain subjects to each member of the team rather than planning together on all subjects, so everyone knew the subjects they needed to plan.

Since starting my new school, I currently have my PPA at home (for which I am extremely grateful) and do my planning then; however, in previous schools where PPA was done on-site, a lesson planning game changer for me was **planning during the holidays**. This is something that a former colleague told me when I started primary teaching, and it revolutionised my life. Spending some time during the holidays to create great lessons takes the pressure off, as I can carefully prepare well-thought-out lessons that address misconceptions and logically map out what I want my pupils to learn. If the school has a clear curriculum plan that is not subject to change mid-year, I can plan a half-term's worth of lesson planning in advance. I tend to **batch** my planning by focusing on one subject at a time, as I find it easier for my brain to focus on one thing rather than switching between different subjects. If you have started in a new school or are working in a school that is undergoing a great deal of change, then you may prefer to plan as you go along, initially to avoid potentially wasting valuable time on planning lessons that may not be used.

I have the lesson details figured out in my PowerPoints; therefore, I do not write lesson plans unless I am compelled to by the SLT and, even then, I rarely refer to them because my PowerPoints double up as lesson plans. I'll never understand why schools continue to pollute the business of teaching and learning with redundant tasks that dull your appetite for the job. So, how did I go about planning during holidays? I'd wake up early, around **05:00 or 05:30** then shower, change and head to my office with breakfast bowl and herbal tea in tow and start lesson planning. My family knew when I was lesson planning and would do their best to avoid disturbing me. If the **weather forecasts** were good, I would change my days of work to accommodate some fun in the sun! I would have some radio on in the background as I work better with a bit of background noise, but you may prefer to work in silence.

Principles of Lesson Planning

During these days of planning, my husband would take care of the food most of the time; if he couldn't, I'd batch cook, or I might order a few semi-healthy take away meals to maximise my lesson planning time. I wanted to restrict planning to a set number of days so that I could square the lesson planning away and spend the rest of the holiday entirely switched off from work. During the summer holiday, I didn't mind spending four days of the holiday planning but, with shorter holidays, I would be disciplined and ensure that planning was done within two days. I'd even work the weekend preceding the start of the holiday or work late into the night to get planning done (oh what a glamorous life I lead!), if necessary, to have a full holiday. Due to a large bank of resources developed over the years, I can recycle some of my planning so that I am not creating plans from scratch, but I still endeavour to improve my planning year on year.

Some people leave planning to INSET days. If you're fortunate to work in a school which allocates considerable time to do this, you could wait till then and collaborate more closely with your colleagues; however, in my experience, there is never enough time to complete lesson planning during INSET, and training days often leave me feeling drained of energy due to the sheer amount of information you're expected to take in on the first day back. In life, sometimes you must **invest time to make time**, and planning during the holiday really helped me with this; otherwise, I would have struggled to maintain a life outside of work.

I prefer planning at home because I have all my textbooks and creature comforts as well as reliable Wi-Fi. I can make myself a cuppa, change into my comfy clothes, work in the garden when the weather allows and there is less distraction. You may prefer to take yourself out of the office and head down to a coffee shop or library for a change of scenery.

Deciding on venue and time is down to you but once you have worked out what your lesson planning preferences are, you're half-way there. Lesson planning during the school holiday does not sound appealing, and it might not be everyone's cup of tea but it's something you may wish to try if you've never tried it before.

Top Tips: You may find *Rosenshine Principles* useful in supporting your lesson planning, as it structures learning in small steps so that pupils are better able to engage with their learning and remember it.

Mechanics of Lesson Planning
Count the Days

If you are lucky enough to work in a school which provides its staff with an academic calendar detailing all school events across the year, woohoo! Once you have this in your hand, you can look at it in conjunction with the school's curriculum overview and count the teaching days. By doing this, you will eliminate surprises and ensure that you have mapped out coverage in the best way possible. In the next section, by way of example, I am going to take you through the specifics of practice that I use to generate lesson ideas for English.

The Rationale Behind the Plan

Before buckling down to serious planning, I **refer to the National Curriculum** (I use the *National Curriculum Parents Complete Guide* from Rising Stars because it is easier to digest than the original framework) and look at the school's **whole-school curriculum planning to firstly determine what the rationale is behind the curriculum overview and how it links to the National Curriculum (NC).** I also find the NC outcomes useful for generating success criteria for lessons.

Sequencing is vital in lesson planning. If you have the freedom to sequence strands of the curriculum the way you wish, I strongly suggest that instead of doing narratives in KS2 at the start of the year in English, which is so often the case, do poetry instead. When I did this, the quality of writing was excellent and because they'd mastered figurative language so well in poetry, they were confident in applying it to more advanced genres, such as narrative writing.

This is a tip that I picked up from a senior teacher in a school where I worked years ago. The **rationale** behind this is that poetry covers a key writing skill: **figurative language**. Figurative language applies to many other genres, especially narrative and persuasive writing, and poetry is a lovely entry point for the exploration of figurative language. It is also a gentler, more motivating way to begin the year, especially for reluctant writers.

Unfortunately, teachers don't always have a choice regarding what is taught when; therefore, an early unit of English for which I had to plan recently was Year 5 'Descriptive Writing', not poetry. I can see from the whole-school plan that the next unit is narrative writing which will last five weeks, so I am already thinking in my mind that I want my descriptive writing to provide a **strong foundation** that will **support** and allow my pupils to seamlessly **transfer** their skills to narrative writing, such as 'show not tell', personification, pathetic fallacy, etc.

Generation of Ideas

When I am planning, as well as considering the important elements that make up the unit, I think about the end result which, in this case, is the composition of an independent piece of descriptive writing. I consider the knowledge that I will need to impart for them to apply the skills taught to be successful: the rationale behind the plan. For example, if I were teaching instructions, I would need to teach features of instructional texts, such as imperative verbs, bullet points and adverbs as well as share real-life instructional texts.

I decide that I want to stick with a **running theme** as **constant repetition** will support pupils' memory of the subject matter. The basis of description for this unit will focus on mystical monsters which means I will refer to this theme throughout. In some schools, the curriculum may be book-based; therefore, the running theme would be the book under discussion. Generally, children find mythical beasts interesting, and pupils will have the opportunity to describe a monster or creature in their independent task. Using a theme will allow for continuity and expose pupils to **subject-**

specific vocabulary throughout, so when they do finally write independently, there should be a lot less head-scratching and blank-page syndrome from pupils. Once I am clear about the direction I wish to take for the unit, I think about how to structure the lesson in order to make learning **clear**, **meaningful** and **memorable**.

For this unit, I visualised the following ideas to ensure success and quickly jotted them down on an **A3 piece of paper**, as I find mapping out lesson ideas easier on large paper. It gives me plenty of space to scribble and I know that these notes are only for me at this stage. Here are some of the ideas I generated:

- **Memorising a text** – Using Pie Corbett's Talk for Writing approach, I will write my own or find an effective short WAGOLL about a dragon/beast/monster which the pupils will memorise to internalise an effective descriptive piece. Once pupils have internalised this, they have a framework from which to work. I look at NC exemplar texts to see if there are any available. In the lesson, pupils will have ample opportunity to verbally rehearse and carry out paired choral work to ensure that this is committed to memory.

- **Adjectives** - I will provide pupils with another monster description that they will up-level (improve) by using precise high-quality adjectives, using a similar structure to what I used in Chapter 7. As a class, we will practise this first with short sentences about monsters and such. I will also share some cluttered sentences to show pupils what not to do as well as examples of tautology (*tiny, little* baby) and redundant adjectival usage (The big, grey elephant swung its tail).

- **Understanding complex sentences** - I will provide step-by-step guidance on this using the monster theme. Dissect sentences. Pupils to write in full sentences.

- **Introducing similes** – Ask planned question about similes. Share examples of similes and get pupils to tell you why the example is a simile. Guided Simile practice, using the monster theme.
- **Exciting verbs** – Define what a verb is. Focus on how the monster moves. Include adverbs.
- **Synonyms** – Will need to encourage pupils to use synonyms for their monster; otherwise, they might repeat 'monster' multiple times in their writing.
- **High-quality visuals** of monsters to support descriptions. Video clips of beasts in film.
- **Independent writing outcome** – Quality not quantity.

I already know from my own observations and data, the pupils with specific accommodations for whom I need to make reasonable adjustments; for example, Guided Writing sessions, gap-fills, word banks, sentence generators, talking tins, etc.

I did consider introducing metaphors but decided to leave them out, as I want the children to be fully versed in similes and adjectival usage before moving onto more advanced figurative language. The **SPaG** elements of the unit will be woven into the **body of the literature** provided and be made explicit in **starter**, **models** and **Shared Writing** opportunities. My starters tend to be procedural so that the focus is on learning rather than pupils trying to work out what to do. This means that there is momentum and calm from the outset. I don't want to begin a lesson with a starter that is too elaborate and takes too long to explain. I have found the termly SPaG starters from **Vocabulary Ninja** to be effective because they provide challenge in a simple format so that pupils know what they are expected to do straightaway. I only paid £10 for a year's worth of SPaG starters, which I think is a bargain! The slides are organised according to term, and they provide pupils with practice in one skill area each week; for example, daily 'Synonyms and Antonyms' starters will have the same layout and instructions but different content. Pupils immediately know what they must do, and this type of high-value procedural system allows for consolidation across the week and maximises learning time. Having routines frees up pupils to think about content. In my early days of teaching, I used to include a variety of 'fun' starters, such as interactive games, wordsearches and the like, but I noticed that these activities did not always sufficiently consolidate learning and usually took longer to explain than to do.

I do not expect pupils to write a story or lengthy piece of writing every lesson; rather, the children will write a section a day and focus on **structure and quality as opposed to quantity**. In essence, when it comes to teaching and learning, **doing fewer things well** is key. What you don't want is learning becoming a mile wide but just an inch deep. If your school adopts the 'Talk for Writing' approach, then towards the end of the unit, pupils will be expected to produce a piece of extended writing independently but, by this point, pupils will have had the opportunity to internalise and memorise a text, innovate (adapt) a text and invent their own piece. I do use some of Pie Corbett's 'Talk for Writing' techniques, particularly for certain genres, such as non-chronological writing, instructional writing and persuasive writing for which Corbett provides some accessible, ready-made short texts for internalisation, but for narrative, diary, epistolary and poetic units of work, I prefer to use the medium of a topic or book that the pupils have been reading. If you can find an interesting hook for your children to latch onto that serves as the **golden thread** stitched into your lessons, it really does help to embed rich subject-specific knowledge which allows pupils to manipulate content with greater dexterity, creativity and imagination.

Now that I have envisioned a unit of work, it's just a case of **atomising** each stage of the individual lessons. I know what I am looking for at the end of the unit but how am I going to get the pupils there? I can't assume anything; for example, once when I was teaching persuasive skills in the form of leaflets, it became apparent that some of the pupils didn't know what a leaflet was. I will need to be granular by crafting or finding models, including precise vocabulary, and structuring it into a well-sequenced PowerPoint presentation. I have my aforementioned textbooks at the ready and laptop open so that I can search online for monster description passages.

Below is a breakdown of an early unit of work on description in English, which I thought would be more helpful than including a maths unit because many primary schools now use bought-in school-wide schemes, such as *White Rose* and *Maths – No Problem!*

English Planning for a Unit of Work Example / Descriptive Writing / Duration: One week

It's time for some serious clicking and clacking of the keyboard! Let me show you how the ideas I previously generated will translate as a lesson plan. Again, I have recycled some of the ideas from my Transition Day (Chapter 7) to show you how you can re-use materials to consolidate learning.

Lesson 1: Area of Study – Adjectives

1. I try to concentrate on the skill rather than the outcome in the lesson objectives because then the children know what they are aiming for. Here is the learning objective:

L.O.: To recognise the importance of **precise** adjectives.

S.C.:

- I can use adventurous adjectives by avoiding 'banned' adjectives, such as small, big, scary, to create specific, vivid images for the reader.

The success criteria are also an opportunity to remind pupils of the 'Banned Word' section of my English Working Wall. Pupils record the L.O. in their exercise books.

2. Next, I insert a Vocabulary Ninja **SPaG starter**; in fact, nearly all my English lessons begin with a SPaG starter strongly linked to

the lesson. Due to the copyright, I can't list them here; however, here is an example of what this could look like:

SPaG Starter - Adjectives

The adjectives in the grey box have been jumbled up. They are adjectives that could be used to describe feeling **fierce**, **confident** or **intimidating**. Can you sort the words under the correct pink words? Look up their meaning in your dictionary, if you need to.

fierce **confident** **intimidating**

frightening	furious
menacing	self-assured
vicious	threatening
wild	domineering
feral	positive
ferocious	savage
untamed	violent
	daunting

I have deliberately chosen adjectives that could be applied to a terrifying monster. I have also colour-coded the words **pink** as part of my SPaG system (Chapter 4). So, from the outset, I am preparing the pupils in relevant adjectival usage as well as **synonym building**. I am always trying to advance pupils' vocabulary through the repetition of language in subsequent lessons and the rinsing and repeating of vocabulary in different contexts.

For the learners for whom presentation is a barrier to progressing, copies of the adjective box in A5 format or smaller are provided so that they spend time on learning rather than expending their energy on the presentation. They write the initials **F** (fierce), **C** (confident) and **I** (intimidating) by each adjective.

For Stretch and Challenge, I ask pupils to record other adjectives of their choosing for one of the words in pink.

3. On the following slide, I display my already prepared **answers**. By inserting answers in advance into your PowerPoint for SpaG starters like this, you save yourself some marking time and pupils receive **instant feedback**. You can, of course, correct in live time but writing each word neatly under the relevant headings slows the lesson down. It takes time to insert answers into a presentation in advance but is well worth it because it keeps the momentum of the lesson going.

To make links with the previous spellings, I will ask the children if they can remember the adjectives that they have been studying in spellings. In my case, the students have been learning -cious words. Wherever possible, I try to find **consolidation and retrieval practice opportunities** in my planning so that the learning sticks well in their minds.

4. The starter gives pupils an idea as to what adjectives are as well as synonyms but, during this stage of the lesson, I want to briefly elicit from pupils how they would define the word 'adjective' and then explicitly explain what adjectives as well as synonyms are. For these definitions, I copy them from *Help Your Kids with English: A Unique Step-by-step Visual Guide* by Carol Vorderman and type them into my PowerPoint.

5. I insert a video about adjectives from BBC Bitesize https://www.bbc.co.uk/bitesize/articles/zy2r6yc with a view to maintaining the engagement of pupils with another opportunity to consolidate.

6. I am expecting at this point that pupils will know that adjectives describe nouns and can add mood to a piece of writing. With this in mind, I decide to insert some images in my PowerPoint for pupils to **verbally** describe the mood/atmosphere. The images I finally decide on are a party picture and raging sea image.

7. To sum up mood/atmosphere, I insert two short extracts which show how adjectives can transform the mood. I bullet point each extract to fade in one-at-a-time. I was inspired by the cartoon character Angelica from the *Rugrats*.

Dark, threatening, frightening mood

Angrily stomping, Angelica tossed her threadbare rag doll aside and loudly entered the classroom. She was truly intimidating. The weather outside appeared to mirror Angelica's foul mood. First, booming rolls of thunder could be heard in the distance, quickly followed by dazzling bolts of electric-blue lightning which consumed the sky.

Bright and cheery mood

Skipping happily into the classroom, Angelica gently placed her beautiful rag doll on her desk, carefully pulled her chair and smiled sweetly at her teacher. It was a fine day. The sun peered through the windows and the cheerful chirping of birds could be heard in the background.

8. During lessons, I nearly always distribute my Sentence Type Laminates; therefore, this is factored into my planning automatically. You can find different versions of Alan Peat's Sentence Types online and adapt them to suit yourself.

9. Next, I include shared writing with keywords to support writing. I also tell pupils to consider sensory language: taste, touch, hear, see and smell.

Keywords

- eyes
- jaws
- wings
- claws
- movement
- similes (advanced)
- synonyms for monster

The keywords give pupils a starting point and clearer understanding of how to build up a picture of the monster in the reader's mind and encourage the generation of high-level vocabulary. The sentence generator I have planned for this learning opportunity is:

> With each pounding step, the ferocious beast...

During whole-class Shared Writing, I encourage pupils to record their ideas in their General Notebooks (GNBs) because Shared Writing serves as a springboard and gets the creative juices flowing. In your school, you may call GNBs by another name, such as draft books, rough books or editing books. Following on from the Shared Writing and magpieing of vocabulary, pupils will complete a description passage of their own using what they have discussed and their prior knowledge. My lesson approach generally follows the three-part structure: *I do, we do, and you do.* You may know it as other names, such as: 'initiate, model and enable' (Jane Considine) or 'imitation, innovate, invent' (Pie Corbett).

10. For the independent task (approximately 30 mins), pupils complete their own description in a similar manner to the 'Shared Write' in their exercise books. This lesson is a baseline lesson to determine how well they can write without a cloze writing frame. In terms of **differentiation**, I organise pupils in a mixed-ability seating arrangement so pupils can help one another, and pupils will have access to sentence types, a pre-prepared word bank based on *Descriptosaurus Supporting Creative Writing for ages 8 – 14*, sentence starters, and perform a Guided Writing session if necessary. Once pupils are all in a state of flow, my TA and I will do live marking and circulate. More fluent writers are expected to be original, using similes, exciting verbs, and a range of adverbs.

Top Tip: If you find that your differentiation strategies are not working, do seek advice from your SENCO or TA. All the TAs and SENCOs I've ever worked with have always been approachable, kind, helpful and knowledgeable.

11. Providing ample opportunity for pupils to self-evaluate and edit their work is a key part of my English planning. Pupils will proofread and edit their work with an editing pen (some schools use different colours for their pupils, such as 'Purple Polishing Pens').

Given that adjectival usage is a key aim of the lesson, I will also ask pupils to underline the adjectives in their work with a **pink/red** pencil. This links to my English Working Wall colour-coding and helps pupils to remember essential parts of speech:

- blue for nouns
- pink for adjectives
- purple for adverbs
- green for verbs

12. For the plenary, towards the end of the lesson, I will ask for volunteers or ask specific pupils to showcase their work under my visualiser to carry out WWW and EBI. I call this 'Celebration of Success' as this is a positive way to end the lesson and gives pupils a chance to learn from their peers. This again consolidates the knowledge learned in lessons and allows for the sharing and improvement of written work.

13. The traffic light slide is displayed. This is a slide that I can quickly copy and paste into my slideshows as it is a regular fixture of my lessons. Pupils highlight the L.O. by writing R, A and G into the letter 'O' or have a sticker to colour-code. (Please see Chapter 5 for the picture of this).

14. As part of your planning, it is vital to reflect on the lesson to improve your teaching practice for the enhancement of learning. This does not need to be laborious as I quickly write my own thoughts about the lesson and pupils' work in my A5 page-a-day diary and will tweak the next lesson, if necessary. Another way of evidencing pupils' outcomes is to take photographs of pupils' work across a range of abilities.

Lesson 2 - Similes

1. Pupils rule off their previous work and record date the learning objective. If pupils haven't acted on teacher feedback from the previous lesson, I quickly add a note to the PowerPoint or main whiteboard to remind them.

Principles of Lesson Planning

L.O.: To understand how similes add interest to descriptive writing.

S.C.:

- I can use similes confidently.

2. SPaG starter which is an adjective recap. Consolidation, consolidation, consolidation! I like to reinforce learning through the recycling of prior knowledge.

This SpaG starter focuses on the identification of adjectives (Spot the Adjectives). In order to stick with the monster theme, I decide to write five graded sentences containing a wide range of adjectives – some of which they will have encountered in the previous lesson. I put these sentences into a *Microsoft Word* file (as shown below). Pupils will have a copy stuck in their books.

> a) Slowly, the amazing beast lifted its large body across the stone-cold floor.
> b) Sneakily, the magnificent beast hauled its immense body across the oak floor.
> c) Pounding the hard ground with its razor-sharp talons, the fearsome creature suddenly launched its sinewy body into the heavens above.
> d) Raging loudly against the villagers, the domineering monster first swivelled its leathery, emerald-green body and then narrowed its luminous yellow eyes, staring intensely at the frightened onlookers.
> e) Without warning, the terrifying dragon scorched the ground with mesmerising fire power.

By formatting into a grid, I can save on paper by fitting eight grids onto A4 and then cutting across with a guillotine.

For the starter, pupils are expected to underline, circle or highlight the adjectives in the monster-themed sentences. You may notice from the starter that I try to avoid beginning sentences with '**The**' as I want to encourage my pupils to open their sentences in varied ways, as this will help them going forward in their writing. As in the first lesson of the unit, I display the answers in the next slide for pupils to self-mark with their editing pens.

3. On my discussion point slide, I ask the following question: What is a simile? I also highlight the spelling of the word to pre-empt misspelling as the word 'simile' is often spelt 'smile' by children.

4. On the next slide, I insert the dictionary definition for the word simile from *Help Your Kids with English: A Unique Step-by-step Visual Guide* by Carol Vorderman.

5. Given that the theme of the unit is monsters, I insert the following question into the slide: What animal similes have you heard of? (Expect responses, such as: As sly as a fox, as strong as an ox). I explain that these similes are regarded as clichéd because they are used repeatedly and that I would like them to write similes which create vivid imagery.

6. **Practice**: On mini whiteboards, pupils create similes for the images shown; for example, rain against a windowpane image could produce the simile: 'The rain hammered against the windowpane like bullets from a gun.' You can decide on which images you wish to use but, for accuracy, I would suggest using photographs rather than Clipart to create a stronger image.

7. **Independent Task:** I share ten differentiated sentences to be completed with a simile; for example: a) Spider's web was as ... b) The long queue looked like... c) His throat was as dry as a..., etc. Pupils are then expected to write similes about the monster they described in the previous lesson.

8. After traffic lighting and the completion of the task, encourage responses from the class and follow the plenary, finishing routines as before.

Lesson 3 – Verbs

1. Pupils rule off their previous work and record the date and learning objective. If pupils haven't acted on teacher feedback from the previous lesson, I do the same as in Lesson 2 above.

L.O.: To include high-quality **verbs** in a short description.

S.C.:

- I can be ambitious in my vocabulary choices.

2. SPaG starter which is linked to synonyms. I provide some boring verbs: 'walk, look, go' and ask pupils to come up with better alternatives on mini whiteboards.

3. Pupils share their ideas, and we write them on flipchart paper which will serve as a poster for our classroom working wall.

4. **Shared Writing:** I share a description of a monster featuring limited vocabulary. We work together to up-level it, highlighting verbs by highlighting in green, as well as the other words within the text.

5. **Independent Task:** Pupils are given a similar task to the 'Shared Writing' and convert the boring description into something more exciting. For my less fluent learners, I will do a Guided Write. The TA will support the MA and HA pupils and then we will swap roles.

6. **Quickfire plenary on synonyms:** I will share a range of verbs and adjectives on the PowerPoint and pupils will give better alternatives; for example:

- small   (Possible responses: miniature, diminutive, tiny, minuscule).
- look   (Possible responses: observe, notice, spot, peer).

I will then end the lessons as explained previously.

Lesson 4 – Complex Sentences

1. Pupils rule off their previous work and record the date and learning objective. If pupils haven't acted on teacher feedback from the previous lesson, I repeat as explained above.

L.O.: To understand the development of complex sentences.

S.C.:

- I can identify complex sentence features used in a text.

- I can develop complex sentences of my own.

2. **Starter: SPaG starter** from **Vocabulary Ninja** linked to adjectives and verbs to be glued into books. Afterwards, we go through the answers.

3. **Guided Practice:** Using the monster theme, I take my pupils through a step-by-step process on developing sentences by using the monster Grendel in Michael Morpurgo's *Beowulf*; for example:

- Grendel darted across the forest.
- Grendel darted across the **dense** forest. > (adjective)
- Fiercely, Grendel zoomed across the dense forest. > (imaginative verb and fronted adverbial)
- Fiercely, Grendel zoomed across the dense forest, which was spooky and eerie. > (subordinate clause to add detail).

And so on.

4. To reinforce, as a class, we perform a human sentence. Volunteers go to the front of the class, each bearing a whiteboard featuring each of the words of your sentence, for example:

Grendel darted across the forest.

Other pupils participate by going up to the front with a relevant word of their choice on their whiteboards and inserting themselves in between their classmates appropriately. At the end of this exercise, the original sentence should have massively improved.

5. **Independent Task:** Pupils write complex versions of sentences provided by the teacher and finish off as explained previously.

Lesson 5 – Invention Writing

1. Pupils rule off their previous work and record the date and learning objective. If pupils haven't acted on teacher feedback from the previous lesson, I type a quick note into my PowerPoint to remind them.

L.O.: To use descriptive writing skills.

S.C.:

- I can use complex sentences.
- I can use fronted adverbials.
- I can use exciting verbs and precise vocabulary.

This is the lesson where pupils will have the opportunity to put all the skills learned this week into practice. They are going to write a detailed description of a frightening dragon.

2. I share a beautiful image of a monster from **Pobble 365**, which is a site that I mentioned previously, with sensory labels to generate vocabulary from pupils. As a warmup, I provide pupils with a WAGOLL on the PowerPoint, and I ask them to tell me what works well, etc. Afterwards, I give them a short success criteria list to guide their writing:

Success Criteria:

- sensory language
- use effective adjectives, verbs, similes
- complex sentences
- proofread

Top Tip: You could even make this a creative writing competition that could be judged by your year team colleagues to further motivate the pupils.

This is just one example of the thought processes behind my lesson planning and how these are translated into planning a unit of English. When planning, ensure that every task has a clear learning purpose. In the past, I have been guilty of creating exciting slides with funky animations and PowerPoint wizardry as well as 'fun activities' for the purpose of pure engagement but, on reflection, these activities added no value. On the occasions that I do use videos and games, there is a valid reason for doing so; for example, in my maths Transition Day lesson, I had a differentiated game of noughts and crosses which consolidated skills learned.

I hope my lesson breakdown will provide you with ideas on how to create well-sequenced, successful and memorable lessons which will stay with your pupils.

In a nutshell:

1. **Planning should not be done on the fly; it is better to be a pristine planner! Start your planning with the end in mind.** What do you want pupils to learn and why? How will you teach it? Break it down into **constituent** parts and get the **details worked out**.

2. **Consolidation** is the name of the game to make the learning stick. Do you want a captive audience? If you stick to familiar structures and repeat key language, more learning can be achieved because less time is needed to explain tasks and your class will be more engaged from the get-go.

3. Keep your lessons **purposeful and invest in some good resources from which you can formulate good planning.** Don't bloat your planning with 'fun' but meaningless tasks.

Principles of Lesson Planning

Notes

Chapter 9
Watchful Eyes

Let's face it, scrutiny in the classroom is never comfortable, even for experienced teachers but if conducted correctly, observations can play an important role in a teacher's continuing professional development. Early in your career, don't be afraid to try and test different learning strategies as this will develop your teaching practice. Hopefully, your school has an observation cycle which is clearly communicated and sets its teachers up for success. If teachers' growth is of utmost importance, there needs to be candour, trust and clear communication between the observer and observed (particularly during formal observations) with a clear focus or foci for development. Schools generally do not formally observe more than three times a year, but many schools will informally observe their staff in some guise or another: informal drop-ins, book looks, governor visits, school tours for parents, learning walks, unsolicited 'support' by SLT, etc. Some schools have more than one person observing to ensure breadth of monitoring and a greater degree of objectivity. It can be rather disruptive to have a constantly revolving classroom door but nowadays schools wish to make themselves available to the entire school community and unannounced visits is something you must learn to manage.

When I first started teaching, SLT would discuss targets to focus on before the observation lesson and give you an exact time slot for your hour-long observation. You would also know who was carrying out the observation, but this is not always the case now; in fact, it would appear that certain schools seek to heighten anxiety by not giving exact time slots or the name of the observer in a misguided attempt to keep teachers on their toes (hopefully, this is not the case for you). In one school where I worked, I was so excessively scrutinised (over forty times during my first year) that it reached the point that unannounced visits no longer fazed me. I'm not sure why the school felt the need to dish out observations like confetti as nothing derogatory was ever found during their observations of me. I would like to point out that this is the only school in my entire teaching career that this type of monitoring happened, so I'm hoping that it was just a one-off unique case.

It is perfectly natural to feel apprehension when being observed by colleagues or external visitors, such as the dreaded monster that is Ofsted, but it is possible to be observed as teachers and not crumble under the weight and torment of nerves. Here are some of my tips on quelling those nerves and getting the most out of lesson observations.

Daily Practice

If you teach **good** or **outstanding** lessons all the time, you have nothing to fear. Striving to teach good or outstanding lessons as part of your daily practice will provide you with ample opportunity to refine your teaching and secure a strong foundation. If you try to coast and get by, you won't improve your teaching skills.

It is also important that you are **confident** in your **subject knowledge** and **daily practice** because, as the saying goes, "Excellence is a habit." Think of every day of teaching as an opportunity to rehearse and improve. If you don't seek self-improvement and don't evaluate your day-in-day-out teaching, how can you become a better teacher? Being self-critical is essential in any field of work. There are some teachers out there who only pull out the 'big guns' when others are watching but I don't understand this approach as they are doing a disservice to their pupils and cheating themselves out of professional growth. Moreover, when observers or inspectors question the pupils during the observation, pupils will say things, such as: "We never usually have this kind of lesson. Usually, the teacher just gives us a worksheet to do." This will signal to your pupils that you don't teach well unless someone is watching and that you don't care about them. If observers cotton onto this kind of approach, it does not go down well. If you know that you need to significantly develop your practice, seek support and observe other teachers. I learned more about teaching and learning by seeing lessons in the flesh, so to speak, than from any book or blog; for example, during my secondary PGCE induction week, I shadowed a student for an entire day and learned so much about the student's experience as well as the teaching and learning across various subjects.

Don't Look!

This may appear rude but **avoid looking at observers** when they are in the classroom as they generally remain impassive and humourless throughout, which is why I smile and remain human when I observe fellow colleagues. Although I do not watch observers watching me, out of curiosity, I do **take note of the pupils with whom they spoke** to ascertain what was said between them later. During observations, I focus solely on the children; I am not interested in gauging SLT or Ofsted's opinion of my teaching from their inscrutable demeanour or being a performing seal to satisfy them. If the children are actively engaged, happy and learning, that's real success. If I can see that the children are not understanding what I hoped they would, I deviate from the plan and adapt because it is important for teachers to **be flexible** to cater to pupils' needs; this is part and parcel of being a teacher. Unfortunately, some observed teachers let their nerves get the better of them and they rigidly stick to the plan they devised, even if it clearly isn't working.

Another area that is sometimes forgotten because of nerves is **pace**. Sometimes, nervous teachers second-guess themselves and think that they haven't explained well enough and go into a repetitive loop of long-winded explanations, or they cram in **multiple activities as a proxy for pace**; it **doesn't work**. It is important to keep the pupils in a state of relaxed alertness and to provide pupils with sufficient time to work through activities. For example, I know from experience that for extended writing, my pupils will usually need approximately 30 minutes.

Build pupils' confidence by asking lots of **planned questions** to assess understanding. Pritesh Kaichura, a London science educator, discusses questioning in detail in his blogs and videos if you're interested. Start with low-stake retrieval questions, then up-level questions with cues in the question stems to support understanding.

Ensure that you leave time in the lesson for a **final plenary** as this is an opportunity to review the lesson's learning. Although your lesson should have understanding checks throughout the lesson, it is important to recap the lesson at the end. I have seen lessons with rushed plenaries or no plenaries at all. Again, this gives the impression that you haven't planned the lesson sufficiently well enough to consolidate pupils' learning.

A good lesson does not necessarily have to be all singing and dancing with an animated PowerPoint and interactive web-based activities. I use the PowerPoint to display key tasks and visuals, but I also make use of the visualiser for modelling effective writing skills, whiteboards for understanding and flipcharts for vocabulary generation. Technology can be great but don't be too reliant on it because it is sometimes at the most inopportune moments that it will fail. I prefer to use familiar tried-and-tested high-value tasks which can be displayed on paper or PowerPoint because they free pupils' mental capacity so that they can spend time on content as opposed to scratching their heads, working out what to do.

In short, when it comes to lessons, observations or otherwise, stick with what works for you and your pupils, and **know your stuff**. Show enthusiasm when delivering lessons and it will rub off on the children. If you're flat, stumbling over your words and not making good eye contact with your class, your lesson is unlikely to be successful. Prepare your resources in advance and don't fall into the trap of shoe-horning interactive games and the like, just for the sake of it. If the activity doesn't support or add anything to the learning, don't do it. You might want to spruce up your lessons a bit, such as cosmetic touches to worksheets or PowerPoint but you shouldn't have to rewrite your lesson.

Feedback

Although rare, there are occasions when you'll wonder how the observer who is inspecting you has ever been allowed to inspect anyone, given their teaching shortcomings. If this resonates with you, I urge you to be receptive to feedback because some of these senior leaders recognise their own failings in the classroom yet appreciate what a successful lesson looks like and have strengths in other areas; in which case, their feedback will be along the lines of 'Do as I say, not as I do'. In summary, not all teachers practise what they preach.

If your school has a planned, well-sequenced **observation cycle** in which you can share with your observer what you would like to develop before your observation, this can be great for your teaching practice as you can discuss strategies with your observer or you could watch colleagues who are experts in your area of weakness beforehand. If you do visit classrooms, don't gossip or comment on the practice of colleagues as it is a privilege to have access to others' classrooms. Some schools are more insular in their teaching practice and do not welcome the open-door approach; therefore, if you are given free rein to observe other teachers, I suggest that you seize this opportunity.

Back to feedback – feedback should be provided in a timely fashion and any criticism should be constructive. Be receptive to feedback whether it's overwhelmingly negative or positive. If feedback is less specific than you would like, feel free to gently request more detailed feedback during your feedback session together. If you recognise the aspects of the lesson that were less successful in the lesson and make this clear to the observer during your feedback session, they will appreciate that you can reflect on your work and evaluate your own strengths and weaknesses, which means that generating areas to improve will be easier. Trust, clear communication and candour are of utmost importance in a mentor-mentee relationship. If you truly are not happy with the judgements, do not become angrily defensive or get into a heated discussion as it often an exercise in futility. In essence, **you can**

either accept the observer's feedback or not – no-one can force you to agree with them. When signing the observation pro forma, you can write an addendum about what you disagree with in an objective manner. Make sure that you receive a copy of the observation form for your records and chase it up if you must.

I had some less than good observations in my very early days as a PGCE student, but I did not allow these observations to define me. I took on board feedback that I found useful and disregarded the rest. Also, I think it is important to note that not all observations or inspection reports are worth the paper they are written on. Furthermore, with all that is going on in our world right now, calamitous events, such as war, fires, hurricanes, floods, climate change, it is important to retain perspective and take what our day jobs throw at us with a pinch of salt.

I want you to know that even if you continue to experience numerous butterflies in your tummy, bite your nails to the quick or twitch nervously before an observation or inspection, it is possible to come through the other side of an inspection or observation unscathed, if you routinely prepare and practise your craft.

In a nutshell:

1. **Know your stuff!** Develop your subject knowledge and make each teaching day an opportunity to **flourish, learn and grow.**
2. **Stick to what works** in your day-to-day practice. Don't be tricked into trying unfamiliar activities in observation lessons. If the task or activity does not add anything to the learning, don't use it.
3. **Be receptive** to teacher feedback as more often than not, it is helpful; however, if you have strong reasons for disagreement, you can **choose to accept or not accept observation feedback.** Remember, not all judgements are accurate reflections of what occurred in the classroom.

Watchful Eyes

Notes

Chapter 10
Meetings: The Thieves of Time

INSET, parental meetings, school meetings and training sessions *should* be **short**, **sharp** and **focused** but, often, they aren't. Despite the title of this chapter, I am not anti-meetings or INSET days. Staff meetings of any kind, when delivered effectively, allow staff to mingle (which creates a strong sense of belonging), share good practice, discuss developments in education and evaluate the school's vision for the future. Training days should provide leaders with the ideal opportunity to set out their stall by setting their expectations, injecting positivity and raising the energy and enthusiasm levels of their team.

In terms of INSET and other developmental meetings, I have experienced the good, the bad and the ugly. One of the worst types of INSET is when, after a full-on day of being generally talked at and told what must be done in order to satisfy certain criteria (usually, but not always, exclusively connected to Ofsted), I am often left with nothing more than heightened blood pressure and a long-lasting, throbbing tension headache. I understand that for some of those leading INSET, many have not been at the proverbial chalkface for several years, but does this mean they develop retrograde amnesia, too? After the term break, it is a shock to the system to be confronted with information overload, a bloated agenda packed with the minutiae of new teaching methods, IT systems, and routines which have never even been touched upon until said INSET day.

Time, a commodity that is extremely precious to teachers, is grossly overlooked as some INSET days run from 08:45 until 15:00 or later. Where is the time to set up or finalise classrooms, collaborate with colleagues about planning or prepare photocopies? Furthermore, in the late afternoon, my brain is frazzled, and I am far too fatigued to do much more.

Before I became a teacher, I worked in several different environments unrelated to teaching and can honestly declare that the first day back at work in those workplaces was never as gruelling as certain INSET days that I have experienced upon my return to school in September.

What can SLT do to make the return to school a gentler, less stressful and more enjoyable experience for staff? After all, happy staff is key to staff retention and should lead to happy pupils. One of the easiest ways in which SLT have a better chance at retaining staff and supporting teacher **wellbeing** is by giving staff **time** to spend on what is truly important: **the practical business of teaching and learning**. Some schools provide well-meaning gifts of appreciation, such as key rings and chocolates, which are wonderful gestures; however, I believe that time is the best and most meaningful gift you can give as a school leader. A component of Ofsted's current framework focuses on staff wellbeing; providing staff with additional time during **school hours** would immediately be a tick in the 'wellbeing' checklist for Ofsted.

SLT also need to be mindful of the language they use in this regard and be quietly generous when providing time to staff by not virtue signalling, as this will only seek to raise the hackles of teachers; for example, headteachers who publicly announce, "I'm being generous in providing you with an extra session for writing reports," or "I am being extremely generous in giving you extra time to do this as not many other schools do," is not endearing, especially as many teachers work incredibly hard, working excessively and ordinarily going above and beyond what is deemed reasonable in most people's minds. Please allow me to share what you should steer clear of, if you are leading a meeting or training session, and what you can do to make meetings manageable if you are on the receiving end of less than satisfactory sessions.

Staff Meetings/Training

If you have a long meeting or training session bolted on to your working day, ensure that you bring snacks and a beverage because not all schools offer refreshments during long staff training sessions. I always bring my laptop because whilst waiting for others to arrive, I can tweak or review my slides for the following day. Sometimes I bring a handful of books to mark as there is nearly always some dead time before training commences.

- Arrive promptly, be polite and respectful to the speaker as it is not easy speaking in front of an audience; however, if the meeting is excessively long and boring, don't prolong it by being the audience member who relentlessly asks questions! Your colleagues will not thank you for it if you do become the inquisitor.

- Bring your laptop so you can type notes directly on your laptop as it easier to word-process than write by hand. Ensure that you leave room at the margins and between paragraphs so that you can annotate by hand when you print your notes off. Reviewing your notes afterwards and writing your own scribbles will help to embed what you have learned during the session. If you prefer to write by hand, ensure that you have a notebook, diary or binder with paper to record any important information. I would also suggest that you record the date, name of the speaker and topic for your records as future employers always want to know what kind of CPD training you have had in the last five years.

- Those in education often talk about differentiation and the concentration span of their students but what about staff? Are staff not learners, too? Adults lose attention just like children. Capturing an audience's attention during INSET means that speakers should provide information, which is **short**, **snappy**, **interactive**, **informative** and **memorable**. There is no point in presenting a breathtakingly beautiful

PowerPoint which fails to deliver its aims and yet it never ceases to amaze me the number of INSET speakers who perform in this way. Monotone speakers who lack passion and display long presentations with densely packed slides are often the reason why staff fail to fully engage with training. To present in a memorable way, speakers need to be dynamic and stick to salient points. In my experience, too many speakers/instructors waffle, waste time and rely too heavily on their PowerPoint presentations. If you are leading a session, you need to brutally edit your presentations as audience concentration wanes considerably, especially at the end of a working day. If you are leading a meeting or training session, think about how you learn and remember to cater to different learning styles – just because your audience is composed of adults doesn't mean that they will retain everything that is presented to them in a "death by PowerPoint" presentation. In lessons, we would never dream of bombarding our students with copious amounts of information in one sitting without breaking it up into manageable chunks, yet this is exactly what some school leaders, external trainers and keynote speakers do to their audience, often reading off their slides verbatim. Adults need to be kept engaged, just like students, and a lengthy PowerPoint tagged on at the end of the day will not be regarded favourably and will likely lead to your audience desperately trying to keep sleep at bay.

Good Practice

In one school where I worked, many aeons ago, a member of SLT was extremely succinct and used a discreet 30-minute timer to keep him focused. If he finished earlier than his allocated time, he didn't rabbit on in attempt to hold us prisoner, he just finished early and released us. I find this culture of "I have two hours to fill; I must fill them" rather bizarre and wasteful. On the occasions that he did use PowerPoint, his slides were basic and only featured images or slides with a maximum of three bullet points; they were never densely populated with text. He did not present swathes of text whilst he was speaking, which meant that we focused on what he was saying rather than reading the slide on display. If he needed the text as a prompt, they were animated so that he was able to introduce one point at a time, which meant that he remained focused on the point he was making. This **focused our attention,** and we **retained** what he was delivering with **relative ease** because he was able to engage fully with us rather than reading from a lengthy PowerPoint.

Disciplinary Meetings

Although I have not personally experienced capability proceedings or disciplinary matters, there are a few things that I would suggest for any kind of grievance from either party. Please see the list below:

- **Keep a detailed written record** about what has been said or done, including date, time, location, person(s) involved, etc. Do not type any details on the school computer as most school devices can be accessed remotely. Avoid writing your grievances in a notebook whilst at school, in case your notebook gets lost; instead, record what has happened on your **phone** whilst the details of the event/incident are still fresh and then this can be forwarded to your **personal** email via your phone or written up in a **personal** notebook at home.

- If the issue has not been resolved to your satisfaction or you are extremely concerned, **contact your union** for advice. Not in a teaching union yet? Join one now!

- If you are called to a meeting by governors and the headteacher, and not a given clear reason for being summoned, ask what the purpose of the meeting is so that you are not ambushed. Before the meeting proceeds, ensure that **minutes** are taken, and that you record what has been said in the meeting yourself. You should also be given a copy of the minutes. Your union may even suggest that a union representative accompanies you to such meetings.

Parental Meetings

If you have a good rapport with your class, send positive messages to parents about their child's progress, and are doing your job well, parental meetings are usually painless as many parents are supportive, kind and helpful. That being said, there are some parents who can make life difficult by unconsciously or consciously projecting their insecurities onto their children, being deliberately difficult, anti-social, anti-school or something in between. This means that you will sometimes have to conduct difficult conversations with an individual who may not be receptive to you or the school environment.

If parents contact the school office, requesting a meeting with you, do ask the office what the purpose of the call is as they should be acting as gatekeepers, narrowing down the reason for calls. If the parent is mysterious, it could be because their reason for contacting you is of a sensitive nature but, ordinarily, it is not, and the school office should be helpful to both you and the parent so that you can fully prepare for the meeting. Once a request for a meeting with you has been set, ensure that the parent is given a specific time slot, including the meeting duration, to stop the meeting becoming a long-drawn-out affair. Also, arrange to see the parent as soon as possible as potentially challenging conversations should not be put off, because problems will fester.

For all parental meetings, not quick messages at the door about dental appointments, record the **telephone conversation (most schools have a system for this)** to record the content of the meeting. If the parent is historically known to be troublesome, kindly ask for a colleague to sit in so that they can be an extra pair of ears. The colleague does not need to be seated close to you; they could be inconspicuously doing work of their own in the background.

Key Points to Remember

1. **Prepare** in advance; for example, if the meeting is about academic needs, you might wish to provide some resources or share with the parent, such as copies of textbooks, weblinks or examples of what is being studied in class to give the parent an overview of what learning looks like in the classroom. If the meeting is about misbehaviour, you could share some information regarding incidences which have occurred – it could be that there are patterns of misbehaviour; for example, days of misbehaviour coincide with something outside of school. If you do share incidences with the parent, for reasons of confidentiality, ensure that you **do not name any other children** involved; instead, say Child A, Child B, etc. The parent will usually recognise who you are talking about, but it should not come from you.

2. Ensure that there is a **'Do not disturb' sign on the door**, in advance, so that the meeting is not disturbed.

3. **Be hospitable**. Ask the parent if he/she would like something to drink.

4. **Carefully listen** and write down what the parent is saying, not forgetting to make **eye contact periodically** (be careful not to stare at them).

5. Be as **warm** and **patient** with the parent as possible, even if they are riling you.

6. If the reason for the meeting is due to the problematic behaviour of the parent's child, **do not dwell on the child's negative traits for too long;** state the facts clearly and concisely, and remember to share the child's positive traits as no-one wants to hear someone perform a character assassination of their child, even if they know their child is no angel.

7. Ensure that whatever points you wish to make are covered, as a conversation should be a **two-way** process.

8. Try to stick to the **time limit** you set as you are a busy individual with other priorities, too.

9. **Do not get into an argument or heated discussion;** postpone, if necessary.

10. Discuss a way to **resolve** the matter and follow up, if needed.

11. Ask the parent if they are satisfied with the '**looking ahead/ plan of action**'.

12. End the meeting on a **positive note**.

Bear in mind that most meetings held with parents will focus on pupil progress, supporting pupils with spellings and multiplication tables – matter-of-fact meetings as opposed to difficult ones. Hopefully, engaging in difficult conversations will be few and far between for you, but the above pointers will give you an idea of how to approach such challenges.

Some schools have clear policies in place that outline a Behaviour Code of Conduct policy for both pupils and parents. A successful school pays due regard to staff health and wellbeing, and recognises that teaching is already a stressful, emotionally charged profession that places its members under enormous strain; therefore, a well-managed school will not wish to add to that because it is detrimental to staff morale and can lead to issues with staff retention. For example, if a parent needlessly and relentlessly complained and bombarded the school with emails, letters and telephone calls; was disrespectful, unreasonable or aggressive; repeatedly failed to recognise their child's wrongdoing; behaved in an entitled manner, such as making demands and telling staff how to perform their role; and persistently absorbed staff's time, then it would be the responsibility of the headteacher and governors to have a meeting with the parent concerned about their conduct. Certain schools go as far as to bar parents if they do not fall in line with the school's code of conduct. Unfortunately, not all schools take this stance but **enduring extremely difficult parents** should not be 'part of the job' and I suggest you try not to allow this kind of indoctrination to seep into your psyche. Any headteacher that places the onus on you or other staff to deal with such an individual is not showing a duty of care.

In a nutshell:

1. **Don't prolong long, boring staff training sessions by asking questions** that you could simply *Google* or ask later.

2. Get into the **habit of record-keeping** for both positive and negative matters, but especially negative matters as initial niggles could escalate.

3. Be **composed** during difficult conversations and ensure that you are well **prepared** for such conversations.

Meetings: The Thieves of Time

Notes

Chapter 11
Assemblies

At some point in your teaching career, you will be called upon to deliver assemblies – both school and class assemblies. This could take the form of secular assemblies or faith-based collective worship. If you are fortunate enough to work in a school where SLT take ownership of school assemblies – great, but increasingly, schools expect classroom teachers to deliver schoolwide assemblies throughout the year. No-one can deny that delivering an assembly in a large hall can be daunting, but I think assemblies are a great way of introducing yourself to the whole school and I have had many pupils who I didn't know come up to me in the playground to say they enjoyed my assemblies; therefore, it is an opportunity to connect with other children (who you might teach in the future) and establish yourself within the school by raising your profile. Composing and delivering assemblies was not something that was even touched upon during my teacher training, which is why I felt compelled to write this chapter because I suspect that assemblies are still not given much attention in teacher training.

When writing this chapter, it got me thinking about the hallmarks of a great assembly. For me, the best assemblies have left me with a warm, fuzzy feeling and have not been interminably long. They have sometimes moved me and given me food for thought. Assemblies are not lessons but they share key features; namely, they have a **clear message**, are **catchy** and **memorable**. So, how do we create and deliver assemblies? Below is my approach to writing and delivering effective assemblies.

Preparing for General Assemblies

To keep me on track, I tend to use PowerPoint slideshow to support my assemblies, but this is not imperative; for example, for one assembly I delivered, I had one slide on display which served as a title page for the theme of the assembly, but I needn't have, it's just my preference. The crucial thing for me when being tasked with writing and delivering an assembly is to write a script with picture prompts as this serves as a comfort blanket, should technology fail. I try to commit as much of the script to memory in order to make eye contact with the audience and deliver as polished a performance as possible; doing this builds my confidence. Stage presence is key in delivering assemblies; therefore, you need to remember to **project your voice** and **warmly greet** the entire school or year group. If this situation fills you with dread, try delivering your performance in private to a mirror first. Practise in your head at the moments of dead time, such as at the photocopier, in the supermarket, etc.

Again, I use a PowerPoint template for assemblies which follows this basic outline.

1. Welcome page with a link to some peaceful music for entry.
2. Engage slide - A clue is provided to hint to the school what the assembly is about.
3. Title page which shows the school what the assembly is about. This could be a wordle or picture.
4. Dictionary definition slide about the theme of the assembly.
5. Elicit from pupils what they know about the theme – instruct pupils to turn and talk to the person next to them for a few moments. With my hand in the air, I use the phrasing: "When you're ready" to get their attention back.
6. Story linked to the theme – This story could be read by me; acted out by some of my pupils (generally speaking, pupils are always happy to help); or a video. I always have a hardcopy of the story I have selected in case the video link does not work. As humans, we enjoy listening to stories as

part of our old oral traditions; therefore, stories are baked in our DNA.
7. Elicit from pupils the message they took from the assembly.
8. Reflection or inspirational quotation in a secular school. For collective worship in a Catholic or Church of England school, I might use a more religious prayer.
9. Thank you for your attention.

Top Tip: During Covid, many headteachers uploaded their assemblies to their school website, so you could use these as a starting point to adapt or craft your own.

Websites that you may find useful for ideas:
SPCK Assemblies https://www.assemblies.org
Assemblies https://primaryworks.co.uk

Preparing for Class Assemblies

I always try to be original and write my own assembly script for my class because you don't want your assembly to be a carbon copy of what someone else has already pinched from the internet! Furthermore, it is important to include some of the work that pupils have done in lessons; for example, in one of my assembly productions, pupils sang a song about the Vikings that they learned in history (this was inclusive because it involved all of the pupils); dance routines learned in PE were included; pupils read their personification poems about Viking ships; and another pupil allowed his *Beowulf*-inspired story to be dramatized by a small group of pupils. I have also displayed photographs of pupils' work in assemblies to showcase examples of great work.

If you have to deliver an assembly at the start of the year, then hinging an assembly on pupils' work could prove difficult but pupils could still learn a song, do a news report and add a short drama scene.

In my written script, I number the narrators and actors; for example:

Narrator 1:
Narrator 2:
Actor 1:
Actor 2:
and so on.

I colour-code stage directions in blue and bold text that requires emphasis. I also insert a helpful reminder at the beginning of the script as below:

During assembly practice, everyone must be helpful, patient and co-operative to give the best performance possible. If we can do this as a class, assembly practice will be an enjoyable experience for all. Please make certain that you keep this photocopy safe and learn your lines.

Once I have written the script, I have it photocopied and provide each pupil with a copy. During the first reading, I ask for volunteers for the numbered parts; anyone who has not volunteered will have what's left over. I annotate my copy to show the names of the pupils allocated to each narrator/actor number and instruct pupils to do the same in pencil. If I can tell that the section selected by a pupil is too difficult, I will break it up into smaller parts or gently steer them to another line. I also check with pupils if anyone has appointments on the date of the assembly as this will mean that they can't have lots of lines. I also assign two PowerPoint slide changers to navigate the slides and play the music links; these pupils are often those who are good at computing. From the outset, I encourage pupils to take responsibility for their class assembly, which usually works well.

Most pupils take great pride in their assigned roles and learning their lines; however, if certain pupils find it difficult to learn their lines, I suggest they copy their text out on a piece of paper which can be backed onto card as this is sturdier and looks tidier than a piece of paper.

For class assemblies, I make corresponding PowerPoints which contain the following slides:

1. First slide contains a hyperlink for entrance music; the music played links to the theme.
2. Whilst this is playing, I display other images related to the topic; for example, for a Viking assembly, I showed images depicting the raid on Lindisfarne, Viking ships, warriors, settlements and Valhalla until everyone had taken their seats.
3. The next slide was a title page with a 'Welcome to + the class name's assembly'.
4. Then the remaining slides were photographs of pupils' work or background displays for set design.
5. The final slide was a 'Thank you for coming' page with a link for exit music.

In addition, props are kept to a minimum because sometimes accessing the hall first thing in the morning to prepare in advance can be difficult, as halls are often used for breakfast club mornings or early morning sporting activities.

Be mindful that not all parents will attend; therefore, praise pupils for their efforts and sensitively check in with pupils whose parents did not attend. You may even wish to treat pupils to some biscuits, fruit and squash afterwards (being aware of allergies of course).

Preparing for Celebration Assemblies

SLT will usually carry out Celebration Assemblies on Fridays but, in the event of SLT absence, teachers sometimes do step in.

This is always an uplifting assembly and if pupils have examples of work, I suggest that a visualiser is used to display work across the school. During the sharing of sports news, events, etc., you could ask some members of Year 6 to deliver a speech about what members of the school community have been up to and they could award certificates, too. I saw this used to great effect during one of my supply stints as the pupils delivered their lines with gusto!

It was lovely to see the warm reception the Year 6 pupils received from the rest of the school.

Another tip to energise the pupils during assemblies is to come up with different styles of clapping; for example, Queen's 'We Will Rock You' clap. This is best left towards the end of the assembly for Times Tables Rock Stars or reading awards.

In a nutshell:

1. **Be prepared!** A **good story** linked to the assembly theme is a good starting point.

2. For a teacher-led assembly, write a **script** and commit as much of it to **memory** so that you can fully engage with the audience and feel confident.

3. For class assemblies, try to be original and **draw on your pupils' ideas and work**. Include **different types of performance**, such as singing, dance, poetry and drama.

Assemblies

Notes

Chapter 12
Conclusion

I hope I have given you a balanced view of what teaching is about and what can be done to simplify the many processes involved in teaching. Teaching can be overwhelming for even the most experienced teacher let alone a new teacher, who may have no idea how best to organise a classroom, compose professional emails or handle difficult encounters. I had to learn as I went, sometimes the hard way, which is why I wrote this book to take some of that sting and hard graft out so that you might avoid some of the lows of teaching that I have experienced and embrace more of the highs.

Teaching is not an exact science, and no two classes or schools are the same, but I like the variety that teaching provides and I have always enjoyed working with children (maybe because I am a big kid myself)! Teaching has its deficits and is certainly not an easy profession in which to work, but it can be an incredible and enjoyable experience, too. I have considered leaving teaching on numerous occasions, but it is the only profession, thus far, that I feel is my natural groove. Yes, there are days when you will feel utterly wrung out, cranky and dissatisfied but then, on another day, you have super lessons followed by kind messages from colleagues, parents and pupils about the great work you're doing. I've been lucky to have many cheerleaders who lift me up when I'm flagging.

In short, teaching is a very rewarding and worthwhile profession, but it is easy to get wrapped up in the 'surviving' teaching mentality rather than the 'thriving' in teaching mentality, and it is my wish that this book enables you to thrive.

Appendices

CLASS COVER PLAN

Thank you for teaching my class today. Please feel free to write any comments below:

Time	Lesson/Event	Details and Date
	Class enters	
	Registration	
	Assembly	
	Maths	
Break		
	English	
	Guided Reading	
Lunch		
	Registration	
	PSHE	
	Topic	
	Prepare for home time	
	Home time	

Class Cover Plan Appendix 1

Date:

Hello,

Details in brief:

Could I please request the following as ticked below:
- **Urgent** assistance!
- Ice pack
- Call home
- Temperature check

Thank you ☺.

(Add your electronic signature)

Medical Proforma (Appendix 2)

Appendices

HANDOVER NOTES		
Class:	**Date:**	**Supply Teacher:**

❏ Self-marked work ❏ Peer-marked work ❏ Work checked/stamped/ marked by teacher.	❏ Discussion-based lesson ❏ Instructional-based lesson with written outcomes ❏ Practical lesson ❏ Whiteboard work ❏ Other

Comments:

Additional Information (if applicable):

Supply teacher handover template (Appendix 3)

WEEKLY TIMETABLE

Lesson number #1 Timings	#2	#3	#4	#5	#6	#7	#8	#9
Subject								
Monday								
Tuesday								
Wednesday								
Thursday								
Friday								

Weekly timetable (Appendix 4)

Appendices

Weekly Overview for (+name of subject)

Date: Week 1

Monday	**Tuesday**

Wednesday	**Thursday**

Friday	**Resources**

Weekly Overview (Appendix 5)

Pupil PE Observation Form

Name:

Date:

Reason for not doing PE:

What sport is being taught? What are the children learning to do?	List the key information for how to be successful in this lesson:
Which members of your class are being successful? Why?	What advice would you give to those children finding the activity difficult?
Be prepared to feedback your thoughts to the class.	

PE Template (not my own, author unknown) (Appendix 6)

Class name: _____

Resources

Please...
- ◇ guillotine (around)
- ◇ guillotine (around and across)
- ◇ laminate
- ◇ enlarge - A3/A4
- ◇ minimise – B5

Thank you,

Insert name here: _____

Photocopying Template (Appendix 7)

Year 6 Overview for Week 5: 30/09/24 – 04/10/24

	Monday	Tuesday	Wednesday	Thursday	Friday
	English L.O.: To plan writing by noting and developing initial ideas.	*English* L.O.: To effectively present the main character and convey dialogue and atmosphere in my opening paragraphs.	*English* Lesson 3: Continuation	*English* L.O.: To develop action through effective adjectives and dialogue.	*English* L.O.: To proofread, edit and publish my story.
	Maths (Adapted White Rose slides) L.O.: Square and Cube Numbers Target skills:	L.O.: Long Multiplication	L.O.: Solving Multiplication Problems	L.O.: Short Division	L.O.: Short division using Factors

French
L.O.: To learn how to say what time you study certain subjects.

Music
Continuing with Happy but with the addition of glockenspiels.

Science
L.O.: To describe how living things can be classified into broad groups.
What is a microorganism?
What are the five different categories of microorganisms? Can you name some examples of virus? Fungi?
Key words: microorganism, microbe, fungi, algae, bacteria, protozoa

RE
L.O.: To learn key facts about the Buddhist festival Wesak.

History
Lesson 4: To explain how Britain reacted to the outbreak of war.

PSHE
Global Citizens – differentiating between wants and needs

Art
L.O.: To use proportion and shapes to guide observations and drawing.

Spellings
Hyphenated prefixes

Overview for Colleagues Linked to Your Class (Appendix 8)

Glossary of Acronyms

1. AI (Artificial Intelligence)
2. CPD (Continuing Professional Development)
3. DBS (Disclosure and Barring Service)
4. DIRT (Dedicated Improvement Reflection Time)
5. ECT (Early Career Teacher)
6. GDPR (General Data Protection Regulation)
7. GNBs (General Notebooks for draft work)
8. HA (Higher ability)
9. INSET (In-service Training)
10. IWB (Interactive Whiteboard)
11. KS2 (Key Stage 2)
12. L.A. (Local Authority)
13. LA (Lower ability)
14. L.O. (Learning Objective)
15. L.I. (Learning Intention)
16. MA (Middle ability)
17. MATs (Multi-Academy Trusts)
18. NC (National Curriculum)

19. NQT (Newly Qualified Teacher, which has been replaced by ECT)
20. Ofsted (Office for Standards in Education, Children's Services and Skills)
21. PAT (Portable Appliance Testing)
22. PPE (Personal Protective Equipment)
23. PTA (Parent Teacher Association)
24. SATs (Standard Assessment Tests)
25. S.C. (Success Criteria)
26. SENCO (Special Educational Needs Coordinator)
27. SEND (Special Educational Needs and Disabilities)
28. SLT (Senior Leadership Team)
29. SPaG (Spellings, Punctuation and Grammar)
30. TA (Teaching Assistant)
31. WAGOLL (What a good one looks like)
32. WILF (What I am Looking For)
33. WWW and EBI (What Went Well and Even Better If)

Useful References

1. Voice 21 https://voice21.org/
2. Andrew Tharby's https://reflectingenglish.wordpress.com/author/atharby/page/8/
- Alan Peat Sentence Types (search online for examples used in other schools)
- See 'Assemblies' https://primaryworks.co.uk
- Beowulf by Michael Morpurgo
- BBC Proofreading https://www.bbc.co.uk/bitesize/articles/zpyhtyc#zhgsrmn
- BBC Adjectives https://www.bbc.co.uk/bitesize/articles/zy2r6yc
- Calendarpaedia www.calendarpedia.co.uk
- CGP link https://www.cgpplus.co.uk/
- CGP Maths for Key Stage 2 SATs Practice Papers
- Descriptosaurus Supporting Creative Writing for ages 8 – 14 by Alison Wilcox
- https://www.dk.com/uk/category/dkfindout/
- Flotsam by David Wiesner
- Help Your Kids with English: A Unique Step-by-step Visual Guide by Carol Vorderman
- Help Your Kids with Maths: A Unique Step-by-Step Visual Guide by Carol Vorderman

- How to be Good at Maths Workbook 2 by Carol Vorderman
- Journey by Aaron Becker
- Kapow Primary
  https:// www.kapowprimary.com/?gad_source=1&gclid=EAIaIQobChMIqO6VhK2XiAMV55NQBh2fbwmnEAAYASAAEgIWKvD_BwE
- Kensuke's Kingdom by Michael Morpurgo
- KS2 Comprehension Success Age 9 - 11 by Rachel Axten-Higgs
- https://www.ilovepdf.com/
- Improving Story Writing at Key Stages 1 & 2 by Alan Peat
- Improving Non-fiction Writing at Key Stages 1 & 2: the Success Approach by Margaret McNeil & Alan Peat
- www.instantdisplay.co.uk
- Ken Robinson quote extracted from: https://www.time2learn.com.au/events/flipped-learning-conference
- Literacy Shed https://www.literacyshed.com/
- Maths Shed https://www.mathshed.com/en-gb/
- Maths – No Problem! https://mathsnoproblem.com/
- Microsoft Word Shortcuts https://www.computerhope.com/shortcut/word.htm
- National Curriculum Parents Complete Guide by Rising Stars
- Oak Academy https://www.thenational.academy/#teachers
- Ofsted Reports www.gov.uk/find-ofsted-inspection-report
- Ofsted Performance Tables www.gov.uk/school-performance-tables
- Ofsted Schools www.get-information-schools.service.gov.uk
- Pie Corbett Talk for Writing https://www.talk4writing.com/resources/

Useful References

- PlanBee https://planbee.com/
- Pobble 365 https://www.pobble.com/365
- Pritesh Kaichura https://bunsenblue.wordpress.com/2015/11/08/welcome-to-bunsen-blue/
- Rosenshine Principles https://www.innerdrive.co.uk/blog/guide-rosenshine-10-principles/
- SEND figures https://explore-education-statistics.service.gov.uk/find-statistics/special-educational-needs-in-england
- SPCK Assemblies https://www.assemblies.org
- Target Your Maths series by Stephen Pearce
- Teach Like a Champion by Doug Lemov
- www.Teacher-of-Primary.co.uk
- Testbase https://www.testbase.co.uk/
- The Write Stuff by Jane Considine https://www.janeconsidine.com/jane-considine-TWS-online-training
- Twinkl https://www.twinkl.co.uk/
- Viking Battle Tactics | Learning Made Fun https://www.youtube.com/watch?v=D-NDVhoGjO0
- Vocabulary Ninja https://vocabularyninja.co.uk/
- White Rose https://whiteroseeducation.com/

www.ingramcontent.com/pod-product-compliance
Lightning Source LLC
Chambersburg PA
CBHW040107100526
44584CB00029BA/3851